Master
Keys
FOR MAKING
PROFITS
IN LAPIDARY

**A Complete Guide of Practical Tips and Methods That Can
Help Hobbyists or Professionals
Realize a Splendid, Dependable Income
From Gemcutting**

By Gerald L. Wykoff GG CSM

Adamas Publishers
PO Box 1991
York, PA 17405
1-717-741-2469

Library of Congress, Cataloging-in-Publication Data

Wykoff, Gerald L. 1930 -
        Master Keys for Making Profits in Lapidary
                p.   cm.
        Subtitle: A Complete Guide of Practical Tips and Methods
        That Can Help Hobbyists or Professionals Realize a Splendid,
        Dependable Income From Gemcutting
                Includes bibliographical references and index
        ISBN   0-9607892-8-6 : $19.95
        TS752.5.W94   1993   93-28639
        736'.2'028--dc20   CIP

Contents

PART III

INDEX

Introduction

People historically have possessed a deep, enduring appreciation for beautiful gems. They likewise extend great respect for the talented men and women who have mastered the art and craft of cutting these magnificent products of nature.

For the imaginative beauty that a master gemcutter is capable of creating, lapidary is truly an art form. Mastering the seemingly complex nature of lapidary equipment certainly also qualifies gemcutting as a craft. This combination art-craft represents value and potential profit. To produce an income, though, requires some other talents.

As much as gems are appreciated, it is surprising how many accomplished lapidaries find difficulty in converting their skills to income. Some gemcutters make a fine living from cutting gems, while others—absent the techniques to produce income—realize little from their work. Strange, isn't it? So many people fascinated with the extraordinary beauty of gems and jewelry existing alongside so many individuals able to produce this same beauty and yet they can't seem to find each other.

This book was written for the many lapidaries, both hobbyist and professional, who would like to realize an income from lapidary. A number of markets exist for any enterprising person. It's just a matter of developing a plan and then introducing the work.

What I've endeavored to do in this book is present as many potential market opportunities as possible. Not every market—and market approach— is attractive to every lapidary. Some individuals detest personal salesmanship. They are reluctant to engage in any activity that would expose them to such an undertaking. This is understandable, although non-selling attitudes and successful marketing are questionable as entries in the same sentence.

Look over this book. If you are at all serious about turning your lapidary talents toward profit making then some of the tried-and-true marketing tips and ideas contained herein may get you off on the income journey. It can be quite rewarding.

Gerald L. Wykoff GG CSM

vi

Part I

Profits Await Gemcutters Who Have Planned Ahead.

Yes, gemcutting can produce superb profits.

More than just a few gemcutters are today realizing excellent incomes from their lapidary talents. The profits don't come in automatically and without effort, of course, but profit-making gemcutters are like any other entrepeneur who have found the way to a successful business.

They realized at the outset that cutting alone won't produce a nickel. As a matter of facet, allow lapidary to remain a hobby and it will consume part of your income.

Fortified by this realization, the professionals sat down and thought up a workable marketing plan. In other words, they planned their work. Then they went out into the market place and worked the plan. The result? If the plan was realistic, profits flowed in. If the plan was unrealistic, negative profits *i.e.*, losses flowed in.

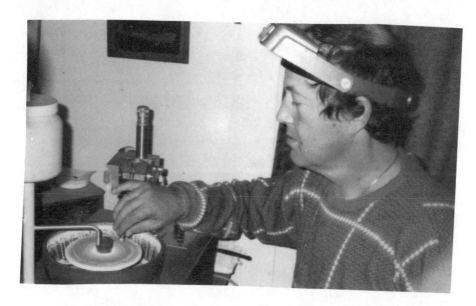

Lapidary is a most satisfying hobby or profession, and it can be made to produce splendid profits...as long as a good selling plan is developed first.

It takes no genius to realize that there is a vast difference between profits and losses.

More than a couple of times as you read this book you will see the expression "...nothing happens until somebody sells something..." That single phrase is the essence of successful marketing and it's what this book is aimed at: making money in gemcutting. A number of highly useful strategies are included in the upcoming pages. They've been included here because they all work...or have worked. They'll work for you, too. First, though, you'll need to put to work the principles behind these strategies.

If you're not now making any or insufficient profits from your gemcutting talents—and you are interested in ending this current stalemate—please know that it's entirely within the realm of possibility. Getting back to fundamentals, there are a few things you have to understand about yourself before embarking on a new marketing plan. It'll take only a few minutes, but take this true or false quiz, to help gain an insight into yourself.

Quick Self Test

1.   I have a clear idea of what kind of gemstone or gemstones I wish to sell: faceted, cabochon, carvings, new Munsteiner or Fantasy type cuts.

        True   False

2.   I have a clear idea of what kind of product I intend to sell: loose, unmounted gemstones or jewelry items where the stone is already mounted in a setting.

        True   False

3.   I have a continuing source of rough or faceted stones so I can continue to maintain a working inventory

        True   False

4.   I am fully capable of going out after sales prospects, making sales calls on other people and engaging in the the give-and-take of personal selling.

        True   False

5.   I recognize that I'm not really the salesman type and would much prefer a softer approach to selling such as mail order, a store, booth, exhibit or some such arrangement where sales prospects come to me.

        True   False

6.   I realize that I prefer to cut gemstones only so I would want to arrange for someone else to carry out selling on commission or salary or a combination of salary and commission

        True   False

7.   I have a good idea of which lapidary items are selling well and what minimum prices I should charge

         True   False

8.   I have a good idea of what group of buyers my primary selling target is: 1. consumers; 2. retail jewelers, repair shops or jewelry designers, 3. gemstone wholesalers; 4. variety, craft or gift shops

         True   False

9.   I know how—or from whom I can get or order—some effective selling tools such as sales letters, promotional literature, calling cards, etc.

         True   False

10.   I have a list of potential customers with which to get my marketing plan started

         True   False

11.   I have decided if I will concentrate in cutting only new gemstones or will also accept repair work.

         True   False

12.   I know what the financial policy of my business will be: 1. consignment or memo sales; 2. pre-payment or payment on demand; 3. invoicing with payment within 30, 60 or 90 days; 4. payment by cash, check or credit card, or 5. commission sales

         True   False

13.   I know if I intend to work out of my house or rent business space to conduct operations.

         True   False

14. I know whether "I'm it" in this business or if someone I know and trust will assist me.

       True   False

15. I know or have checked out any licensing, credentialization or filings that may be necessary to launch a business

       True   False

16. I have the equipment and tools necessary to sustain a professional lapidary business

       True   False

17. I have developed a clear idea of the geographical limits of my intended marketing area: city wide, county wide, state wide, region wide, national

       True   False

18. I know if I will participate in gemstone related shows or exhibits such as: 1. rock and gem shows; 2. mineral society shows; 3. flea markets and or garage/yard sales; 4. national gem shows such as Tucson Gem Week, Jewelers of America, etc.

       True   False

19. I have a firm opinion on whether I will sell traditionally cut gemstones or will go in for the customized, unique, contemporary and/or trendy cuts

       True   False

20. I know that I can cut gemstones at a professional level—or perhaps have even started or completed the gemcutting certification process of the American Society of Gemcutters

       True   False

Score yourself one point for every true answer.If you
score sixteen or more, you're about ready to lunch a profit making
venture right now. If you scored less, you still have some important
planning to complete. Whether you're at the top of your marketing
game or just at the "kicking around a few ideas" level, read on. You
may find some information that will make a profitable difference.

Setting Up a Plan...

The point of the little quiz was simply to demonstrate the im-
portance of hard thinking in fashioning out a marketing plan. Until

**Contemporary research shows that traditionally shaped faceted stones
and uniquely shaped cabochons turn buyers on. Take a careful look at
your stones, and decide if they are truly saleable.**

you have a firm idea of how you'll proceed with your lapidary business, it's best to come to firm grips with your own personality, time available, how you intend to spend your time and money, and to whom you want to sell.

Do you really need to be a glib sales type person to make profits with your gemcutting? Of course not! A reasonable personality will do just fine—borderline misanthropes perhaps will have a hard struggle—because marketing allows for many different types of people to become successful. If the idea of actual selling seems truly repugnant to you, do what other successful entrepreneurs have done: hire sales people.

You don't need to be a glib sales type to make money with your lapidary skills. Good work is still the best sale maker so concentrate on your cutting...and the salesmanship will come easily.

A look at the range of sales possibilities proves that anyone with a plan and perseverance can make money in the gemstone business. The ones discussed in the next few pages don't exhaust all the possibilities. As long as there are creative sales people out there, new ways of wringing a profit will be introduced.

Here then are a number of suggestions you might want to consider as you ponder the profit arena.

Selling to the Trade...

Are you willing to load up your gemstone presentation case and go a-calling?

Many professional gemcutters insist on selling to people who know and understanding gems, who are constantly in the market for well cut gemstones, and who can "speak the language." If this kind of selling appeals to you, take a hard look at the trade.

Further, if you wish to concentrate mostly on cutting—and re-pairing— gemstones by selling to an easily identified market, then the jewelry trade is definitely it...retail jewelers, jewelry repair shops, jewelry designers, and gemstone wholesalers. It isn't hard finding this market: look your waiting prospects up in the Yellow Pages if you must. There's a bonus to working with these business people, too. You are a valuable, additional source and they really do want to talk with you. Nine times out of 10 they'll be available when you stop in or call for an appointment. And every jeweler—if you provide good prices and services and establish a trusting rapport—will fill your appointment books with referrals to friends and gemstone consuming suppliers.

You don't need a lot of slick printed sales aids (although attractive sales literature is extremely effective! **Tip:** See page 162 for a way to obtain expensive, attractive looking four-color promotional literature very inexpensively) and doo-dads to call on a jeweler. Your calling cards are represented by the stones in your case. A jeweler's stock in trade is being able to evaluate good cutting. On your first call, you might not make a sale but if your stones are of professional quality and you made a good impression, chances are you'll get an eventual call.

1982 VOLK

The key to success in trade sales lies in developing as many potential customers as possible. You can very well produce good results with only a jeweler or two. If, though, you set up a schedule of calls and go visiting as many jewelry shops as possible, the orders will even out—yes, work does seem to bunch up at times—and keep your gemcutting equipment busy.

Sales literature is important, of course, but usually you'll need little more than a nice business card. Your stones speak for themselves.

Needless to say, service is paramount when dealing with the trade. If you say you'll have a repaired stone back in the jeweler's hands by Friday, then make certain you deliver on Thursday or Fri-

Do your best work on cutting consistent with the time available to remain profitable. It's a tough call—but you must know when to quit.

day—not the following Monday.

Selling to Consumers...

The toughest—and most profitable—market is selling direct to consumers. It's in dealing with the average consumers that the jewelry industry came up with the truism, "...the gemstone will make the profit but the metalwork will sell the piece..." What that means is that few consumers know much about a gemstone—and they're highly suspicious of any that are sold outside the conventional network. Low on gemstone knowledge, though, a consumer knows s/he is protected on karatage by the Federal Stamping Act and also knows what good goldsmithing looks like. It takes no practiced eye to see a poor finish, a badly joined or fitted seem, a poor weld. Consumers also lack jewelry design imagination so trying to sell loose, unmounted gemstones to them may be extremely difficult.

Think long and hard before you make an effort to market loose, unmounted gemstones, however valuable and quality cut they are, to a consumer. Consumers don't have the industry contacts to coordinate stones, settings, and goldsmithing and they will show you no confidence that they'll be able to figure it out either. At the same time, the average consumer has no more jewelry imagination or creativity that a tree stump and will simply be incapable of mind picturing what a piece of finished jewelry will look like.

If you want to sell to the consumer, consider the wisdom of placing your stones in nice mountings so you can offer a buyer the finished item. That's what a consumer is interested in. They'll "ooh" and "aaah" the beauty of a cluster of polished gemstones—but they'll walk away without buying.

You don't necessarily need to know goldsmithing to produce finished jewelry. Get in contact with a repair shop, get the shop's "trade price list" and hand over a quantity of work. Unless you have the time and talent to develop professional goldsmithing skills, it's better to have a contract shop do the work. Remember: "good metal work will sell the piece." Poor metal work will loose the sale.

Stripped of all the mumbo-jumbo, selling gemstones involves little more than getting the stones in front of a prospective buyer. Wishing won't do it: selling effort will...especially with a plan.

Selling on Consignment...

Consignment or memo selling is tough. Frankly, it's just about impossible—for the average gemcutter. It takes money up front to carry off this kind of marketing, and for the most part, loose gemstones are an intermediate product, not a finished item.

With "no payment until sold" type selling, you put your merchandize into the hands of another, knowing that you won't be paid until the stone is sold. That can be a tough wait. Not only do you have to wait until the stone is sold, but you have a money collection challenge, too. Getting paid money that's owed to you can certainly test your tenacity.

You must invest in the rough, invest time to cut the stone, and then wait until someone else gets around to selling or buying the stone. Yes, most consignment-memo deals have a time limit whereby if the sales entity doesn't sell the stone in a specified period of

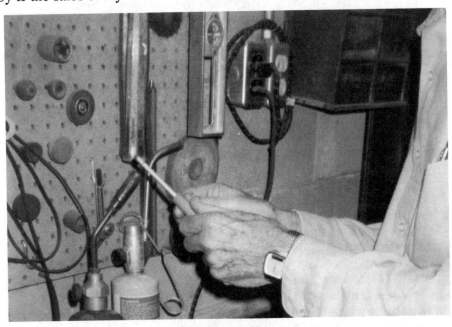

Should you cut gems only or do gold/silver-smithing so you can sell completed jewelry? Probably you should deal with a metal smith and concentrate on your gemcutting talents.

time—say 30 or 60 days—the stone must be returned to you. With contingency selling, you want the stone out there being presented to prospects not back in your workshop. All the time, somewhere between your investment in rough and the time when you might receive money in hand, a lot of cups can spill.

Just keep in mind that before the money starts coming in, you must make a substantial investment for consignment selling...and there's no interest paid on your money.

Who is the best sales partner when considering consignment sales. Many gemcutters attend rock and gem shows and set up liaisons with merchants who sell loose stones in their booth. These merchants are often rock show gypsies who follow the promoter around the country, selling and replenishing their inventory. They like a reliable source. Remember, though, that they are human enough to want to buy cheap and sell dear so they'll ask for a major percentage of the sales price...if they don't try to buy the stone cheap outright.

Consider Cutting, Selling Top Quality...

Show merchants are often quite good at agreeing on a sales price for your stones, then retailing them at a higher price and paying you the percentage of the contract price. Best deal to make in such circumstances involves setting a price that you want for the stone and then letting the merchant charge what the traffic will bear. Your prices need to be low, too. These people deal with Far and Middle Eastern suppliers where excellent lapidary work is cheap, cheap and plentiful.

Before continuing on the subject of consignment, let's pause a few moments to consider some aspects of the type of gemstone you'll be trying to sell. The mere fact that these capable foreign cutters are in position to challenge your selling plan should give cause to think out carefully where you are going with your gem sales. Cheap labor almost rules out any possibility of conducting a continu-

Just look at the trays of foreign cut stones at a gem show and you will see evidence of powerful, low cost competition. You must be realistic about these low prices, well cut stones and plan your strategy accordingly.

ing business based on cheap synthetics or cheap natural stones. That doesn't mean it's impossible, just more difficult. You'll be selling few synthetics and poor quality stones to the trade: they have better, cheaper sources than you. With consumers who don't have an effective reach into the lapidary industry, you will probably be more successful with lower quality merchandise.

Lots of people-trust also becomes part of the formula for successful consignment. You have to know and trust the person with whom you're dealing. But memo selling can work—and the key is finding a trade person who is constantly involved in the business making gemstone sales to anyone with an interest.

Selling by Commission...

Commission selling is a close relative of consignment-memo operations. This is the route to take for a gemcutter who doesn't wish to become involved in the hurly-burly of selling.

If you simply want to cut gems but don't wish to sell, find a sales oriented person and "cut a deal." Telling someone to go find a

salesman and cut a deal is easy enough for one offering advice. It's not quite so simple to put into practice. Finding a good sales person takes time and effort and good judgement. If you don't already know someone who could represent you, you'll need to advertise. This can be done inexpensively by word of mouth, telling someone in the trade—a jeweler for example who gets contacted regularly by good sales people—or a gemcutting colleague who may know someone, or mentioning your need to one of your own suppliers. Personal contacts, of course, are best. Failing to find a sales person, the next step is to advertise for one. A classified advertisement in the local newspaper doesn't cost all that much and will probably get you a number of contacts. The advertisement doesn't need all that much in the way of explanation. Here's some wording that you might want to try, or re-write to conform to your own needs:

> "**SALES**—Immediate commission opportunity available for individual w/(or without) experience in selling to jewelry stores. Greater Chicago area. Call 000-0000.
>
> "**SALES**—we need to add solid, commission professional sales person to sell to jewelry stores. Call 000-0000.
>
> "**SALES**—If you are honest, aggressive, well groomed, we have career commission opportunity selling to jewelry stores in Chicago area. Call 000-0000, ask for Fred.
>
> "**SALES GEMS**—Immediate opportunity available for individual w/experience calling on the jewelry business. Greater Chicago me-

tro area. For appnt. 000-0000.

"SALES-GEMS—local gemcutting business needs commission salesman to call on local jewelry trade. Good earnings for low pressure go-getter. Call 000-0000, ask for Fred."

The above aren't the crown jewels of classified advertising, but they do show a prospective salesman that a commission job with the rather pleasant task of calling on existing jewelry businesses is available. Depending on the size of the newspaper and the character of your marketing area, you should get a number of calls from interested people.

With the local newspaper, though, you may not get too many prospects with jewelry industry experience. If you want to advertise where maximum exposure to jewelry industry sales people will see

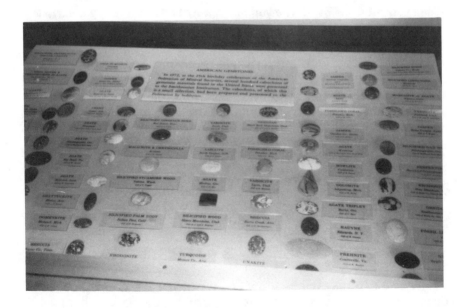

The display of your gems is most important, and often the judicious use of the standard brief case—outfitted with attractive display trays—will be sufficient.

When you cut a fine gemstone you put in work and talent, and you have a right to be compensated for your efforts. Don't discount your valuable work.

your message consider jewelry trade magazines such as Jewelers Keystone Magazine or National Jewelers. Their classified rates aren't all that high and sales people looking for new sources peruse the classified columns every month. Your ad, properly worded, will attract these people—almost all of whom have a wide following in the jewelry trade. You can contact the classified sections of these publications by writing to:

JC-K Classified Ads   National Jewelers
Attn: Eleanor Yap   13760 Noel rd #500
One Chilton Way   Dallas, TX 75240
Radnor, PA 19089
215-964-4462   800-688-7318

The two magazines shown above have two-month prior deadlines. This means that the ad you order in January will appear in the March edition.

Most salesman like to talk, not write letters. They want to respond to a person on the telephone—and they also sometimes like to call COLLECT. Maybe they're truly interested and maybe they're not but shmoozing with you on a free phone call sure beats working. Make up your mind if you're willing to accept collect calls and realize that a cross country conversation for a half-hour or so can add to the telephone bill. My advice is: don't accept collect calls. Many people are perfectly willing to place a call, talk a long time as long as the other guy is paying for it. By making prospects pay for their own calls you can select out those who are truly interested, serious enough to pay for his own job hunting, and assure you that the person on the other end isn't going to waste your time.

You want a sales person who will work for you but also one you can trust. Get references, even the names of a few customers, when you conduct the interview.

When you do get a call, interview the prospect but for heaven's sake find out if h/she is bondable and get references. After all, you will be turning over an inventory of valuable gem stones to this person (most gemcutters don't require bonding although it is a good idea) and you want to be as sure as you can be that the stones won't suddenly disappear. The most common ploy by a dishonest salesman is that his stones were "stolen."

Get the following information on any commission salesman prospect:

1. Name and address and telephone
2. How long in the jewelry business (if already in the trade)?
3. Is s/he currently employed or representing another company?   (**Note:** If you get a confusing answer on this, ask for the names of a couple of jewelers that s/he's called on in the past week—and then call these jewelers and confirm the integrity of the answer.)
4. Can sales prospect make a deposit on first shipment of stones? (**Note:** It's a good idea to make an unknown salesman de-

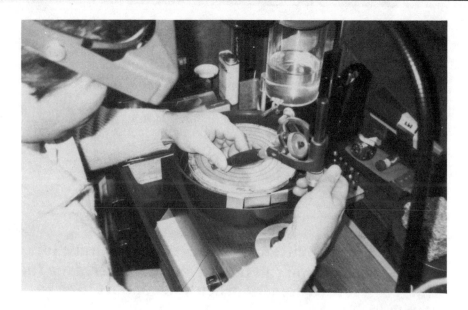

In your readiness to cut for profit, don't overlook the arrangements will have you competing against the Thai sweat shops. They are strong competitors.

posit the cutter's value for the first shipment and continue to do this until you get a confident working arrangement. Keep in rule in mind: it's awful easy to steal gemstones.)

   5. Does sales person have any experience selling gemstones and if the answer is "yes" will your stones be in competition with another supplier? Or is the sales person simply trying to fill out his or her line?

   6. Will the sales person use your trays or his or her own?

   7. Engage the sales person in a conversation about gemstones and find out how much gemological and gemcutting knowledge the sales person possesses.

   If you like the answers, if you believe you have the kind of representative, then go ahead and "cut a deal." State the commission you'll pay and be prepared for a counter offer. You want a low commission, and the sales person wants a high one...somewhere in between lies the "deal."

   Written contracts are pretty much a must in dealing with a commission salesman so be sure and have someone competent draw up the agreements you plan to use.

Have a lawyer prepare a sales agreement covering bonding, payment, delivery, responsibilities of both parties. Yes, have a written contract but remain realistic about its efficacy. It costs a lot of money to enforce a contract across the country, even across state lines. Chances are when push comes to shove you will back away from hiring an expensive lawyer to go after a salesman whatever his violation of the contract agreements.

Because the legal resolution of disputes is so expensive and time consuming, be wary of letting the salesman get into you for more than you can afford...called the "walk away point." A "walk away point" is the money value-loss intersection where you are willing to throw up your hands and tell the salesman "be gone!" You might lose some money and some gemstones in a walk away, but that's better than getting in deeper.

Every jeweler or repairman has an unpredictable need for stone repair, and sometimes a quick telephone call will establish a liaison that can lead to more profitable work once your cutting talents are known.

What are the clue points that you perhaps will enjoy trouble with a sales person? My own experience is this: the first time the sales person gives you ANY kind of unjustified trouble in turning over money that is owe and due to you. The instant that happens, the little bell in the back of your head should go off like a set of chimes—and keep ringing. You should start pulling away...or do a "walk away."

Selling to Specialty Stores...

You'll need some marketing preparations and a good plan if you wish to sell your stones through specialty stores. At the same time, you'll need to come to grips with what the specialty store own- ers' needs—usually it's for finished jewelry.

Experience will soon teach you that loose, unmounted stones are best sold to jewelers, repairmen and designers. Everyone else has

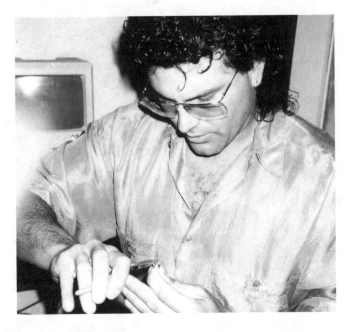

Sometimes, only a minimum of stone setting skills can come in handy on small repairs. It would pay to invest in a pair of stone setting pliers.

trouble coping with a loose stone other than to put it on the coffee table as a conversation item. The exception to this case is the craft or hobby shop where the owner or an employee is able to fashion jewelry pieces, using gemstones.

The profit you'll realize from each jewelry piece even at wholesale prices to the retail dealer will obviously be much higher than marketing loose stones. So, if you do decide to target in specialty stores, make a decision on selling loose stones vs. finished jewelry pieces. Going the finished jewelry route implies a decision on the kind of jewelry you'll produce.

Expensive jewelry involves karat gold and sterling silver. Costume jewelry involves white metal, plastic and paper. Yes, some incredibly imaginative and inexpensive jewelry can be made with paper and gemstones! If you doubt what I say, go to a craft shop and buy a book on making paper jewelry.

When dealing with specialty, gift or small independent stores, realize that the owner-operator will usually want finished jewelry, not loose gemstones. They just don't get the loose stone demand.

Price-wise you want to put the store owner in a buying stance where it's possible for the latter to at least keystone *i.e.*, double the buying price. If the store will retail your article for $5, then you must produce and sell it for a maximum of $2.50. Forget all the tales you've heard about a store's markup at 40%. That just often isn't true with jewelry where keystone is the rule of thumb.

What stores are best? Avoid the chain or franchise stores. The hired managers are rather locked into the chain's suppliers and often don't have the authority to make deals with you (despite their often protestations to the contrary). They're worth a try, of course, but pin your marketing hopes more on the independent store. A small gift or souvenir shop would no doubt love to have an added jewelry line—especially if you agree to set it up on a consignment.

Look over a craft shop carefully before you try to put stones or jewelry in. Often you'll be competing with other jewelry lines. It doesn't hurt to see what the competition is or will be.

Selling in a Kiosk...

Don't overlook getting into an agreement with or setting up a kiosk in a shopping mall. They offer you low rental costs, and many mall operators are willing to allow you in on a test basis. That's an invaluable incentive if you want to do your own retailing.

The warm reception from both customers and mall managers is making kiosk retailing a fast-growing trend in the '90s. Some shopping experts feel that kiosks may represent the wave of the future. Certainly they are a welcome revenue generator for financially troubled malls. Plenty of retailers have simply gone out of business rather than fight the big discount stores so malls need to be creative. The kiosks' temporary leasing contracts help fill in the gap when a retailer gives up his lease and deprives the mall of merchandise se-

Many small malls and strip shopping centers are promoting kiosks with outstanding arrangements. There's a manning problem, of course, but you can make outstanding profits with the right location and product mix.

lection and income.

To combat the situation, malls are coming up with temporary lease programs involving kiosks and these arrangements have risen sharply since their introduction in 1990. What mall operators like about the kiosk is that they bring back mom-and-pop retailing and provide mall customers the personal service that smaller retailers provide.

For you as an entrepreneur, a kiosk allows you to try your hand at mall retailing without the costly risk of going directly into an in-line store. With the cost worry of expensive lighting and display fixtures, kiosk operators are left with more cash flow for operating costs and inventory.

The goal of temporary leasing programs is to act as a breeding ground for retailers who might eventually grow into in-line store status. Make no mistake, though. Getting involved in a kiosk operation is a full-time business committment and someone will have to man the kiosk during mall hours.

If you think a kiosk operation might be just the thing for gem stones and/or gem jewelry, closely examine first the mall you want to get into. Develop a concept or a theme for your kiosk, such as a watch of a "chain by the inch" type kiosk. One you've worked up a viable marketing concept, contact the mall manager. Discuss thoroughly all leasing options becausethey differ in each mall.

Thanks to the already demonstrated value of temporary

kiosks, some mall developers have started to test other creative leasing operations. For example, the "vanilla box" is a small, in-line store stripped of all the fixtures and ready for a retailer to test the "mall waters." Some malls have gone even farther and have created in-line stores with fixtures available for retailers for six to 12 months.

Strip Malls Attractive...

One of the more inexpensive places to consider a kiosk or a vanilla box offering would be in some of the strip malls. Strip malls took a tremendous beating during the '80s and enterprising developers are working hard to come up with a package that will bring back the stores—and the customers who fled to the big malls.

Don't look down your nose at the small strip malls. It's true that most people's memory of a strip shopping center is that of a poor cousin to an enclosed mall. Those little strip malls can be highly lucrative—if you pick the right one with the right lapidary marketing concept. Strips are making a concerted effort to lure back the retailers they lost over the past three years.

Strip malls often offer daily-living goods such as food and counter drugs as well as personal services and specialty items. Their ability to attract retailers lies in the fact that the strips offer lower rents and fewer restrictions than do the big malls, and they attract customers who are more focused on what they want to buy and therefore demand the convenience that malls can't always provide.

The small strip mall attracts shoppers looking for quick, serviceable convenience. A kiosk offering inexpensive ear rings, beads, pendants and rings will often produce suprising profits.

As indicated earlier, if you provide good, fast service in your lapidary store you'll get a strip mall shopper's attention and patronage. Lower rent obviously is a powerful inducement for you to consider. For example, in 1990 jewelry stores paid a median of $12.78

For a fast, profit making kiosk operation, consider specializing in ear rings. You can cut matching stones, mount them—and ear rings make a great impulse purchase. Other jewelry can round out your line.

per square foot to rent in a strip center. Compare that with a median $33.88 at a regional mall. Also, restrictions such as advertising and when the store should remain open are other impositions with malls.

People go to strip center stores to buy, not pass time. They like the convenience of not having to drive a distance to a regional mall, being able to park close to the store, and not having to walk through the entire mall just to find one item.

A strip center jewelry operator can spend more time with customers and have fewer security concerns because s/he doesn't have to contend with the heavier traffic of a mall. Some claim the strip malls attract a better clientele, certainly they attract fewer shop lifters.

Strip center shoppers look for value and quality, and tend to have more price-value confidence in a gemstone seller who is out of the mall rather than in a mall. If you sell on price alone you may find more comparison shoppers in a mall. The downside is: the strip may be in an undesirable area or have an undesirable mix of stores. Both tend to drive good customers away.

But a strip center represents a powerful way for independent

Like other retailing approaches the flea market enables you to try selling stones with a minimum investment.

profit seekers to distinguish themselves from the big chains and attract time-strapped customers who know what they want and how much they're willing to pay.

If you can manage it, this approach is a good one for you to consider. True, in a kiosk or vanilla box you have the challenge of manning the store for long hours. Most malls are open seven days a week and responsibility for having someone on hand can be heavy. They require you to be open during certain business hours whether the manning is performed by you personally, a member of the family, a friend, or an employee. True, it's a full-time committment (and then som!) but it can indeed be lucrative.

Selling in the Flea Market...

Flea markets represent a traditional sales outlet for small discounters who have something to sell and don't want to make a big investment in setting up for sales. They've been so successful over the years that developers have set up outdoor flea markets as well as indoor ones. Some of the indoor ones take on the appearance and operation of a bazaar or modern mall.

For shoestring operators, a booth or space in a flea market can produce splendid returns. It's a matter of selecting a good flea market that enjoys traffic and support. This happy combination isn't that difficult to find. For flea marketing, research often means little more than just spending a day at one of the flea markets in your area and observing the traffic flow, then talking to some of the operators. The latter are usually quite happy to talk with you about the market they're in—as long as you don't talk to a prospective competitor.

For such an operation, you'll face the same conceptual decisions as you do with other markets. Will you be selling loose, unmounted stones or will you be selling a jewelry line of some type? The latter is obviously preferable. With loose stones you're hoping to catch the occasional craft person who needs a stone to make a piece of jewelry. There aren't all that many in a flea market.

Pricing For Flea Markets...

There are, though, a lot of people who are willing to part with a few dollars for a nice piece of jewelry. Generally, trying to sell top of the line, high quality and pricey jewelry won't work in a flea market. Flea shoppers there are searching out bargains. Jewelry at any price is a luxury and these shoppers tend to part with the big dollars in a mall or strip center store.

To operate in a flea market, you need only a sign (often the promoter provides these), a table or two, some table coverings, and a series of trays to hold your merchandise. Make up pricing cards or slips and place them strategically about your trays. Flea market shoppers like such information right out front where they can see it without assistance.

Anything goes in selling at flea markets. If you are so inclined, take a look around the house and find as many old pieces of jewelry as you can find. Always be on the lookout for the unusual. Offering inexpensive gold jewelry can complement your gemstone sales, help fill out your line and make it even more worthwhile for someone to stop and linger over your offerings.

If you need to buy old jewelry and jewelry related items for your flea market operation, consider subscribing to

> The National Flea Marketeer Buyers Guide
> 11565-C Ridgewood Circle
> Seminole, FL 33542
>
> or
>
> Flea Market USA
> 2156 Cotton Patch Lane
> Milton, FL 32570
> Charles and Dorothy Clark

These two publications list new products of special interest to flea market vendors and show information. It also lists suppliers of jewelry and other merchandise. It's a wise investment to subscribe to other publications that are devoted to antiques and collectibles. Check with the local library to see which ones they may carry. Order or buy sample copies of all publications that fit into your area of selling interest. Later, you might want to advertise stones in them.

Helpful Publications...

Plenty of helpful publications exist for a lapidary wanting more information on the flea market where sales of loose stones can be conducted alongside jewelry sales.

You'll also want to hunt out the existing flea markets. A little

Go through the local and metropolitan newspapers for sales opportunities such as flea and garage sales, fund raising events, etc.

research on your part should turn up a number of profitable shows such as the famous Brimfield (MA) flea market (contact J&J Promotions, Rt 20, Brimfield, MA 01010), or the Renninger's No. 2 in Kutztown, PA, every Saturday throughout the year (contact Renninger's, Box 107, Adamstown, PA 19501).

Read your local newspaper. If there are going to be any church fairs, antique shows or other places where all kinds of merchandise are sold, papers will carry stories. Usually, complementary classified or space advertising, too, twill explain where to inquire about participation.

It goes without saying that to be successful in flea marketing you must be ethical, knowledgeable and offer common sense when dealing with customers. As a dealer you are an "expert" to these buyers and they expect you to have the answers to their questions. Try to price your goods competitively and realistically and if the quality of your gemstone merchandise is superior to what others are offering, have confidence that it carries a higher price tag. You'll soon know if your prices are right: the cash box won't lie to you.

The opening and closing days of a show are the biggest from the point of view of attendance. Dealers and collectors get their earliest because they like to "skim." They're the latest, too, hoping to buy at reduced end-of-show prices.

Do comparison shopping at any show you enter. Walk around and check the prices: it's worth the time. The other dealers don't want you to undersell them too much. Dealers buy from each other, allowing slight courtesy discounts to colleagues.

Make your booth distinctive in some way so that it is attractive and appealing. Think about a traffic puller. One profit taking gemcutter in Georgia cut and polished a huge piece of blue glass slag...it looked like history's mightiest blue zircon, blue topaz or aquamarine. It wasn't really for sale—but did it ever do its job of attracting traffic. Another dealer made the World's Biggest Base Fiddle. All it did was stand in his booth—and draw traffic.

Another gemcutter bought cheap, promotion grade faceted emeralds and each day she conducts a free drawing of customers who come to her booth, giving away as many as 30 free emeralds. It

The best display of lapidary goods in a flea market is to lay out the items with easy-to-read price information. Many flea market buyers love to shop by walking up and down the aisles between the exhibits.

really draws heavy traffic—and costs her about $10.

You will also maintain a competitive edge and appear more professional if you distribute business cards. Be sure to include your name, telephone, and business address (it's up to you if you want to be handing out your home address—rather than a box number— and telling people that you have lots of valuable gems in the house!). Another good method of retaining customers, especially if you are a vendor who works different shows and markets each week, is to write down on the back of your card your scheduled locations for the nex few weeks.

Many shows year after year have many of the same exhibitors. The dealer provides the location, booth space, and, hopefully, the traffic. You must provide everything else.

It takes almost no sales ability to conduct a flea market operation...plus this type of marketing is among the least expensive to get into for selling and trying your luck.

Folding aluminum tables (they're nice and light) or card tables work well. Cover the table with something hardy but attractive such as a piece of velvet or plastic cloth in a dark color. If you're displaying good jewelry, buy or make a couple of glass counters or cabinets with glass doors that lock. To keep track of your sales, make out bills in duplicate. If your area has a sales tax be sure that you apply for a certificate and collect the tax.

Plan For Comfort...

Don't forget to bring a comfortable chair or two to sit down on: it gets mighty weary late in the day or under a hot sun (umbrellas for shade!). It gets hot inside even with air conditioning, so wear light clothes inside, appropriate clothes outside. Bring along some sheets of thin plastic to cover things if it rains.

The outside walls or aisles are preferred. For some reason, people often do a complete circle of the outer aisles first and then zig and zag through the inner ones. If the show dealer offers a discount ticket program (so you can hand them out to good customers) be sure to ask for your share. On a multi-day show, plan to take home your valuable pieces of jewelry.

During a show, remain vigilant. Pilferage is a real problem because the out-in-the-open displays invite quick fingers. Do remember to bring bags, boxes and tissue paper to wrap the merchandise once its sold.

A marvelous promotion gimmick at any flea market is the dealer's bargain box. Fill a box with odds and ends, small cabs and faceted stones, and offer them for a dollar or two. People just love to paw around and hunt for a bargain. Keep a good re-supply in a bag under the table. The bargain box must, of course, be left uncovered. A good suggestion for an inexpensive give-away might include some of the promotional emeralds that are available from a number of vendors. The emeralds, of course, are of poor quality but they are faceted reasonably well. As give-aways, you can get a lot of wonderful promtional mileage out of

"Free!   Real Emeralds!   Free!"

A last suggestion: get the name and address of every buyer. This way you can drop them a postcard when you're going to exhibit at a show in their vicinity and thus build up a following.

Selling to Consumers...

One-on-one selling is where you'll find the big profits. It's where you'll find rejection, too. Selling direct to a consumer is the toughest way of all, but the most rewarding, both personally and financially.

When you sell to a store owner or to someone in the trade or from a flea market or in some such environment where the customer has a predisposition to buy...even coming to you...the psychological risks for you aren't so great. Your ego and personality aren't on the line.   Prospective customers either want to buy or they don't. Your function is more akin to an order taker. Order takers don't introduce their emotions into the sales equation quite as much as a direct sales person. That's why the latter are paid so well.

To sell direct to the consumer means that you load your brief case with your wares and go out seeking buyers. Now a salesman has often been defined as someone who sells you something you didn't want at a price you didn't want to pay. That's not what I'm talking about.

> **"A good salesmen finds needs in people—or attempts to evoke need— then sets about to fill that need in the best way s/he knows how. That' s what real direct personal selling is."**

To succeed in direct selling then you must have good merchandise, priced fairly and realistically—backed up by an effective selling plan. The best selling plan is one designed to develop and retain buying customers.

Here's a suggestion for a selling plan that works.

One-on-one selling is the most challenging but potentially the most profitable. The first few moments are critical in personal selling.

Set your selling up using CIPs (center influence people) as the target market. A CIP is an individual who can open up a whole group of buyers for you. Satisfy a CIP and s/he will brag you up to a wide spectrum of friends and associates who know and trust his or her judgement. Good CIPs include nurses, mechanics, ministers, grocery store checkout people, lawyers, waitresses or waiters, officers in organizations, teachers, etc.

Use CIPS For Effective Selling...

Develop a trustworthy business relationship with a nurse and in short order she will introduce you to other nurses, doctors, patients...people with the wherewithal to buy almost your entire lapidary output. Her CIP influence can be extraordinary.

The same impact will be exerted by the other groups mentioned. If you can develop a dozen CIPs, your lapidary business is assured of profits...it's really that easy.

The selling plan is a simple one.

✍   target CIPs by writing down the names of a few people to whom you believe you could sell your wares.

    ✍   set up so you will make sales calls at these designated customer's preferred location.

    ✍   cut a few stones that show your talent off.

    ✍   get brochures and literature from findings and mountings manufacturers. Get the catalog from Tripp's, the New Mexico company that produces pre-notched metal mountings. Obtain a catalog from a discount store like BEST or EVANS which sells a line of karat gold gemstone jewelry.

Search out CIPs if you plan on selling direct and provide such good product, price and service that these influential people will want to "brag you up."

    ✍   load up your briefcase with stones, literature. Make sure you have a few pens and pencils and a sketching pad. Then go a-calling on the first name on your CIP list.

> **"The whole philosophy behind CIP marketing is to provide an outstanding bargain to a key, influential individual and then allow word-of-mouth to take over from there."**

The motivation for this kind of selling plan is to work with your customer toward designing a piece of custom jewelry. You'll need to know how to sketch jewelry (if you can't draw, get a copy of my book, "Master Jewelry Design," and develop a modicum of skill). But the ability to sketch and explain design possibilities to your customer isn't the sine qua non of jewelry selling. You have other, probably superior, techniques where your customer's imagination isn't so vital.

If you must, pull out the BEST catalog and allow the customer to select a design s/he likes. Can you duplicate or design close to that? Is that the idea? Usually, such an approach will pose no problems. Given the support of casting houses from whom you can obtain catalogs, you can easily duplicate whatever selection is made by a customer.

Once you've decided on a design, get a deposit from the customer, order the mounting, cut and/or buy the stone (many designs require diamond accent stones so you should get yourself a wholesale diamond source, too), perform or hire a goldsmith to complete the work. When you deliver the finished item at an attractive price (and one that is also profitable!) you will doubtlessly have a happy customer on your hands. You certainly should have one who will be anxious to spread the good news of her buying triumph—and you will have even more customers to deal with.

A selling plan like this can spread quickly. It just takes a little early seeding, plus nourishment with good work and service and your profits will be assured.

Selling at Conventions...

It's never been a big market, but in the early 1990s it was still lucrative and not especially competitive...for someone selling lapidary produicts. I'm talking about convention selling—which can be extraordinarily profitable.

Selling at a convention can be the same as at a flea market operation (except that you can usually sell higher priced items at a convention) or a specialty type operation. If you want to go ahead with a consistent marketing approach, plan on buying floor space at a local, state or national convention. For example, if you're interested in selling loose, unmounted stones consider the national, state or local dentist's annual meeting. Almost all dentists have training in lost wax casting and they're a marvelous prospective market for cabochons, faceted stones, even carved pieces. You could probably even sell a bunch of waxes to dentists, and a convention floor is a perfect opportunity to talk with them.

They're not great for a sales pitch in their offices. A convention is another matter. I know. I did it with marvelous results.

A convention exhibit space usually is measured in terms of a 10-foot booth. You get the space and guaranteed traffic flow for the fee. In most cases, you must pay the floor contractor extra for carpets, chairs, tables, ash trays.

You'll get your best results if you place your wares on a front table and work with aisle traffic. Many convention goers are somewhat reluctant to go into the booth until there's been a special rapport and trust built up. This rapport generally comes after the convention goer has indicated genuine interest in something specific. That's the time to go into the booth and sit down and complete the sale. Don't expect this two-step procedure to dominate all sales. Sometimes, people see something interesting on the table and buy it on the spot.

Incidentally, check with the convention manager for the association before buying a booth. Recent IRS rules sometimes prohibit actual cash sales on a convention floor by a non-profit associa-

Selling at conventions can be done on the exhibit floor in pursuit of hard, cash sales or as a specialty exhibitor in the sponsoring organizations's hospitalty or registration room. The latter option usually is free, on invitation.

tion or organization. You don't want to make investments and then be unable to conduct sales. The public relations approach may be fine for suppliers to a particularly industry but your efforts are pegged to immediate profits. After all, you're not likely to see these people again unless you become a regular exhibitor. Even then, the visitations may be annually.

Pennsylvania Gemcutter Mixes Traditional With Contemporary

Everyone these days keeps insisting that cabochons must be unique or customized to sell. The old traditional ovals, they claim, won't sell fast enough or at a good price.

True or not?

Not true, says a successful gemcutter, Jeffrey Milland of Palmersville, PA. He's been cutting and selling cabochon jewelry since he was 18 years old. He cuts and sells standard cabs as readily as the new cuts. Standard shape mountings are easy to obtain.

To Jeff, standard cabs are his bread and butter. He buys stock sterling silver, 10K and 14K gold mountings, preferably with a few heads for accent stones. If the mountings are merely oval rims, Jeff has small heads soldered on so he can add diamond, zircon, or white sapphire accent stones.

Diamond accents are used with expensive cab materials such as turquoise, jadeite, lapis lazuli or opal. Less expensive cabochon materials still look equally attractive when white sapphire or river colored zircons are used as the accent stones—and the costs and price are kept low. He has a long list of satisfied clients who appreciate his two-tiered pricing structure.

Jeff seldom cuts a cabochon on speculation. He says that he generally has a firm idea in mind for a piece of jewelry when he cuts gem materials for shape or texture. His favorite approach to cabs is to cut pieces jig-saw style and fit them together. For example, he once fitted a round cherry opal cab dome inside a canary yellow opal standard cab, and has often created "eye" stones by gluing faceted stones into cabochon cutouts.

Spending almost half his time on actual selling expeditions, the Pennsylvania man often has a piece of jewelry sold before he even cuts the stone and mounts it. That's why many of his cabs are standard ovals.

"Look at this traditional vs. contemporary cab shape from a realistic viewpoint," he says. "People are comfortable with the familiar. If I cut a beautiful lavender jadeite oval, mount it in 14K gold with some diamond melee, do you really think I'll have a difficult time selling. The answer is: of course not. Try it with an oval of turquoise and you'll get the same answer. Fine looking piece: easy sale.

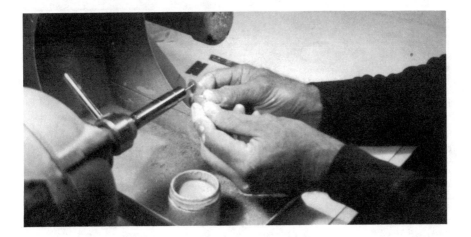

Professional gemcutters invest in specialized equipment so they can cut unusual shapes. It often takes a bit more time, but the investment is returned.

"As for these new Munsteiner, Fantasy and negative cuts, yes, people are excited. I don't know how long this fad—if it is a fad—will last. But an imaginative combination of various stones or cut types and shapes will do the same thing...create buying interest."

With a customer, Jeff sketches up a rough idea of the finished design and gets an OK and deposit. He wants both himself and the client on the same wavelength because surprises cost money and injure feelings. In the actual cutting, his absolutely first step is to study the rough. The stone to him is the feature so it has to be the best he can get from the rough or slab.

You have more influence than you think over a gemstone or

Much of cab strategy involves moving a template over a slab until just the right orientation for texture is visible. Then the outline is traced in.

jewelry buying decision because of your gemological knowledge. It's important not to squander this built-in advantage with a wary customer. He wets the slab and then slides a cutout paper template around looking for just the right combination of pattern and texture. He admits he "worries" over a pattern before marking it out with an aluminum pencil.

To add drama to his display cases, Jeff utilizes different col ored pads. He past es unmounted cabs directly to the pad covering so they'll give the best viewing performance. Later, after a cab has been removed, he glues again over the paste residue from the last cab, covering it up and maintaining a neat tray.

Finally, as an artistic touch he mounts on the inside lid of his briefcace a series of four-color photographs of outstanding jewelry items featuring stones that he cut. This display, he feels, helps stimulate a buying reaction as the customer begins to see—and want to duplicate—the beautiful designs.

Like most successful professional gemcutters, Jeff attributes his success to good bookkeeping, careful buying of rough, successful yield calculations—and hard, constant selling effort. By now, he has an outstanding list of satisfied customers who are quick to promote his name and work. Lately, more and more designers have been contacting him. His ability to do some of the contemporary cuts holds him in good stead with advanced designers.

The Importance of Trust...

How much credence does the average jewelry buyer have in you as a gemcutter when you're talking about a gemstone or a piece of jewelry?

Apparently, you have more influence that you think.

Women buy most of the jewelry in the U. S.

What is the influence that is strongest in her choices? Friends? Magazines? Co-Workers? Other women? Retailers? TV? Movies? Newspapers?

It goes without saying that any ongoing **business relationship must be built on trust. As the saying goes, "bend over backwards" to assure your customers that you will deal with them fairly. The word gets around quickly.**

If you answered "retailers," you're right. In a recent survey of women jewelry buyers it was discovered that the "greatest impact" in the choice of which item of jewelry to buy, the "trusted jeweler" was first.

Some 75% of the women surveyed agreed that dressing fashionably was important, especially for women who work. But the influence on older women selections was not the media or friends, but the ability to see an item regularly in their favorite stores. Women in their late teens and early 20x, on the other hand, are heavily swayed by magazines.

To find the latest trends, mature women depend on their retailer on a jewelry sales person. Only 11% would change their jewelry style from what they see on TV or in the movies.

Effective Marketing Begins With Analysis of Costs...

How much are your gemcutting skills really worth?

For many gemcutters, such a question contains little relevance. For them, faceting or cabbing is strictly a hobby. They made their investment in time, money and energy so they could fully enjoy the remarkable sense of accomplishment and creativity offered by cutting one of nature's most incredible achievements—gemstones.

Others, though, recognize their unique skills as a valuable, marketable entity. They sell—or would like to sell—their efforts and output. Between the two extremes lie many gemcuttersf who do occasionally sell a stone or item of jewelry...and would sell a lot more if they could get a better grip on marketing. To gemcutters who are interested in selling their work, the adventure into selling is often repaid many times over.

Effective marketing of gemstones begins first with an analysis of cost structures plus realistic mark-up. Too many gemcutters take

the position that so long as they own the equipment and operate from their home they are excused form the rigors of overhead planning. Only the hobbyist can afford a lack of cost recovery. For one who chooses to sustain an ongoing marketing profile, overhead costs will exist so long as s/he needs a place to work and use the equipment and material upon which to apply skills.

The "I have no overhead because I work at home" gemcutter will continue to believe s/he needs not figure in these costs of doing business right up to the time that equity has been exhausted and there are no resources to replace equipment or rough inventory, expand operations, or pay for advertising and promotion expenses. That's when a realistic attitude toward over head and direct job expenses comes in handy.

Before moving on to actual marketing practices, it is best for a gemcutter to deal with the basics such as laying down a firm financial foundation so later pricing decisions are pegged to reality. The hobbyist often may feel s/he can establish virtually any price for work without serious danger to income or profit. This cutter works at home. The equipment is paid for. The electricity, lighting and other needs are cost-of-living (not cost-of-business) expenditures which must be paid regardless. Retired people enjoy this luxury.

The true professional knows s/he doesn't enjoy such perks. Such a haphazard approach to cost would lead to disaster. The equip-ment might be paid for, but with each use it's gradually being used up, called "depreciation", and eventually will need replacement. Cer-

Gemcutting as a hobby is one thing. It's something else entirely when you are conducting a professional business and those expensive wheels must be replaced through gemstone sales income.

tainly, there will be a continuing need to replace worn-out wheels, pads, disks, belts, polish and stone inventory. Light, heat, electricity and like must be borne by gemcutting operations and income, and the cost of rough becomes an integral part of the pricing mechanism.

By not covering your "nut," you give away your hard earned equity—and that's a formula for financial disaster. To price your work realistically, you should know your cost structure.

It's not necessary to be a bookkeeper or CPA to do overhead planning. Truth is, it's not all that difficult...merely a business necessity—or go broke.

The first priority of any marketing plan then involves the establishment of your cost base...sometimes referred to as your "nut" or "overhead." You must establish how much it costs to keep you in business NOW and in the FUTURE. Remember: overhead isn't just paying your bills but also in making certain you have funds to expand and/or replace exiting tools and equipment. You must know how much this costs—and also what your time is worth.

Armed with this self-knowledge, you can then determine how much to charge and whether you will approach each job with a "Fixed Overhead Allocation" or a "Sliding Overhead Allocation." Incidentally, some of the most successful fulltime professional gemcutters operate on a "Labor Adder" principle.

"Labor Adder" is Easy to Apply...

In the latter cost estimating approach, the gemcutter assigns a specific dollar amount to the time involved in a lapidary project. That is they assign a specific dollar amount to the hour-time involved in cutting the stone, buying the mounting, setting the stone. To this amount is added a percentage amount of the labor and this added percentage is intended to cover the "nut." With the nut and labor accounted for, the gemcutter now adds the cost of the rough, the mounting, and any expenditure made to finish the setting. That establishes the cost of an item. The markup or profit margin is the final element added.

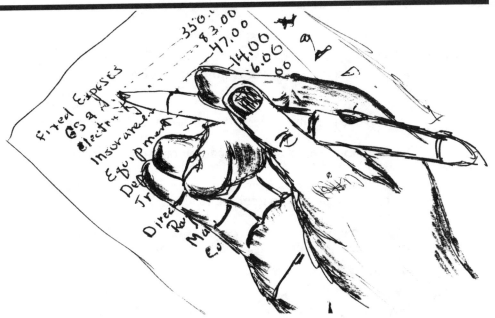

When you cut a gem you invest work and talent and the business has an obligation to return this investment—with a profit. If you do decide to discount your work, accounting will tell you the repercussions of those decisions.

Most accounting systems are not this informal. They provide for the "nut" to be broken down into two principle categories: 1) fixed cost, and 2) direct job expenses (this latter category is also sometimes referred to as "indirect costs." Fixed costs are those costs which arise whether you ever sell a single gemstone or not *i.e.*, rent, electricity, insurance, depreciation, inventory, etc.

Direct job expenses (DJE) are those costs that arise because of the company's work *i.e.*, cost of rough, selling expenses, time and labor to complete work, delivery charges, mounting services. etc.

Take a long careful appraisal of yourself and your fixed cost situation, and review any numbers harshly. Get your house bills out and study them. Get the numbers for the entries below so you can set up a true financial picture of your lapidary business. Only when you have entered and considered all costs that go into keeping your business alive will you ever be sure that selling gemstones for a certain price will cover costs or not cover them.

FIXED COSTS

GS&A (General Service & Administrative) costs
Rent
Insurance
Fixed office expenses (electricity, light, A/C, heat, etc.)

Depreciation (Replacement of equipment and materials)

Labor (Your salary or salaried help as a fixed cost—unless you have a commission operation

Professional Services (magazine subscriptions, industry group dues or fees, gem pricing services, catalogs)

DIRECT JOB EXPENSES

Cost of rough

Mounting or jewelry making expenses (if any)

Selling expenses (Direct mail, telephone, personal calls)
Delivery charges
Time & labor (any labor time directly attributable to the work or jobs)

Know Your Costs...

Where is your workshop? —in your home or are facilities leased or rented? If it's the latter, you have a fixed recurring expense item which must be recovered regardless of the level of sales. Don't fool yourself about your house being free: if you still have a mortgage, insurance, or upkeep payment you're faced with a fixed cost line item.

How about your lapidary equipment? Is it paid for or do you still owe on it? In either case, you have continuing depreciation and/or replacement responsibility. In either case, you have a depreciation and/or replacement situation because continued use will obligate you to buy new equipment, laps, wheels, polish, tools, supplies, etc.

Have you considered business set-up costs? Do you have

business cards, letterheads, printed envelopes and other promotional literature, a business telephone, magazine subscriptions, gemstone pricing subscription service, etc.?

Have you invested in gemological degrees or association memberships? Are you a GG, FGA or a member in any industry groups or associations such as the American Society of Gemcutters, one of the appraiser or federation groups? Your degrees and memberships have great value but they—and other ongoing fees—are still a cost element.

Once you've carefully compiled your list of fixed costs, you'll need to examine the area of direct job expenses. The easiest way to achieve a good understanding of DJE is to regard these expenses as costs which simply would not have occurred had you not accepted the work.

If you count only the cost of doing a job (DJE) you will fail to cover all your overhead costs. With that kind of approach, your pric-

Go over your accounting records regularly so you'll know where the business is profit-wise. If bookkeeping isn't your favorite subject, get a one-write accounting system or one of the simplified computer programs.

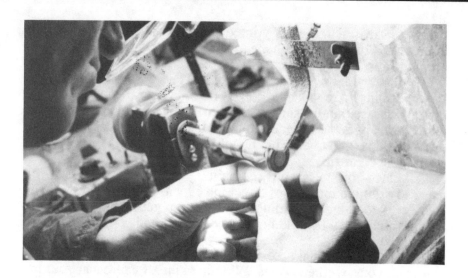

If it takes longer than normal to complete a unique, customized gemstone, then the stone's price should reflect the extra labor that went into its production, regardless of the stone's intrinsic mineral value.

es fail to produce the necessary profit to continue your business. If you have been contracted to cut a pink tourmaline, DJE will arise in the consideration of the rough (whose rough is it?), the time and effort to cut (labor and craft content) either a standard of a custom cut (your expenses should differ for cut design considerations), and any selling, insurance, or delivery expenses. Do you issue an appraisal for your work when selling the complete jewelry item? The cost of doing the appraisal, printing of the form should be accounted for.

Figuring DJE...

Keep in mind that the cost of the rough often represents a prime example of careful DJE planning. For fine rubellite, the rough cost per carat is significantly higher than poor colored, heavily included material—and the final price generally reflects this higher DJE . That's easy to understand, but handing over a finished gem to a customer has less DJE than the need to mail and insure the work. Why? An expensive stone can be quite costly to mail, and you should be prepared to recover these extra costs. Postage can eat a business alive if it's not carefully controlled.

If DJE sounds a lot like "Time and Material and Extra Cost Recovery," that about what is involved—with only slight variations. Your variable labor costs are DJE, but your salary—if you have one—is actually a fixed cost. Think of any service business and you'll quickly come to realize why the business owner may pay his employee $10 per hour but charge you, the customer, at the rate of $20 per hour. Why? The owner must pay not only for the labor cost $10 per hour). He must also pay for insurance, equipment, an office, the telephone and equipment, light, etc., etc. In short, he adds these charges as overhead recovery...plus, hopefully, a small profit for putting all this money and managerial skills at risk in hopes of getting enough business volume to produce a reasonable profit. You should do the same...even if you're the only one involved.

The available business options are rather stark for a business that does not show a profit. They are: make a profit—or else. Hobbyists can survive on equity and professionals can't.

For every hour the employee works in his behalf the owner must recover SOME fixed costs and ALL direct job expenses. But if the employee is doing no work and remains on the payroll the owner's fixed costs remain uncovered. The owner faces three choices: 1) find work for the employee; 2) terminate the employee (which ends the company's ability to perform work and recover at least some of the fixed costs, or 3) go out of business or go bankrupt for not earning enough to pay the employee AND pay for costly overhead, too.

You can thus see why your fixed costs will exert enormous influence on the price at which you sell the output resulting from your talent and effort (after all you must recover your fixed costs) and how else except by working and selling. It's not difficult to understand why many gemcutters get into manufacturing of jewelry itself: it affords a higher income per sale and allows for a greater price markup.

Applying Overhead...

The straight application of overhead—and a method which often proves impractical for gemcutters because of fluctuating output—would mean that you compute your overhead for a certain accounting period (usually a year or a three-month quarterly period). An estimate of the amount of work to be done during that period is then computed (a sales goal!) and a proportionate amount of overtime, in strict ratio to the cost of the job, is applied.

What makes this method so severe is the fact that small stones often can't support a stiff assignment of overhead: it just makes them too expensive. Often you must adjust the price you charge to what the market will bear. It's not likely you'll get a lot of work cutting 3-carat Citrines with an accounting cost of $20/per carat when Citrines sell for $10-$15 per carat retail. The reality of the dealer-retail price structure makes that obvious.

Foreign cutters are good and low-cost so you are forced to set your own price accordingly. This usually means cutting better quality stones.

How then do you establish your time/skill value so that your quotations are still competitive while allowing you a reasonable profit? Keep in mind now, that jamb peggers in Bangkok are fully capable of turning out 150-200 stones per day at a wage scale that is only a fraction of the minimum U. S. rate.

There is a way and it's termed "sliding overhead." The principle behind this cost application approach is that larger, expensive stones can carry a bigger load of your overhead than can the small stones which could become seriously overpriced. Thus you load the big stones, but not too much as to overprice them also.

The mere fact that cutting small or inexpensive stones competitively is so difficult—some say impossible—is what causes many gemcutters to restrict their cutting to custom cutting of valuable materials. This strategy permits the gemcutters to establish more easily a pricing structure that allows them to pay their costs and earn a respectable income form their output.

Using a "sliding overhead" allows you to force the big, valuable stones to carry more overhead than the small stones. This enables you to cover your costs adequately while still pricing stones realistically for the market.

Knowing your fixed cost recovery total, you should have a pretty firm idea of how much to price a stone...or at least you should have a firm number in mind as to your hourly costs. If you know that your time is worth $32 an hour you can easily work out a price quotation on a stone that you estimate will take 2.5 hours. If the stone has an extremely high per carat value, then premium pricing for such a stone is also justified. That's why it often doesn't pay for an American gemcutter to cut agate or jasper cabochons for sale to the trade: you just can't make money at it given the competitive prices form the Mid and Far East.

You can apply this type of pricing on a "per carat basis," or on a "cut stone basis" or on a combination of the two. The next question to arise could be: which approach is best? Should I charge on a "per stone" or on a "per carat" basis?

Many professional gemcutters, for obvious reasons, prefer the cut stone price applicaiton: they want the larger, "custom cut" stone which justifies the higher cutting price and thus makes their time more valuable. It's not unheard of for a professional to establish a minimum price per stone, around $50 each. Can a tiny stone be cut profitably at that price? Of course it can! It can as long as it's a ruby, sapphire, or emerald. Don't try to get that kind of pricing on a Rose de France or an average garnet.

Furthermore, a minimum price on a custom cut bid allows pricing flexibility so the cutter can accommodate a small stone as easily as a large one. Many professionals shy away from small stones—that's cutting standard tinies—on the justifiable grounds that they really can't compete successfully. Even at $25/carat, how much money can you make cutting half-carat round brilliants?

Use Video to Promote Sales...

You can always go high-tech in your stone sales...if you own or can use a video camcorder. After all, Home Shopping Network makes good use of the home TV and VCR and has been showing splendid profits for years by letting people see the offerings.

Carl Childers of Lubbock, TX, took a page from the HMS page.

Here's how Carl, a Certified Supreme Master Gemcutter, does it. He arranges his selection of cut stones and pieces of saleable jewelry and then makes a video tape of the arrangement with his camcorder. Of course, the camcorder records a beautiful full color of the stones as a group. Later, Carl takes individual shots of outstanding pieces.

He doesn't do it all the time, but Carl can make copies of the original video. The next step is easy enough: he arranges for his video to to go out on free viewing loan to his many customers—and those people who are not customers.

The results, to say the least, are dramatic. People view Carl's stones in the privacy of their own homes...without a salesman's pressure. If they like what they see, Carl's name and phone number are included on the video. A sale is just a phone call away.

The video tapes are inexpensive. Carl's home VCR is useful for making extra tapes. The whole operation costs little, provides a great promotion—and makes money. And, yes, the tapes are perfectly reusable.

Part II

Teaching Gemcutting Can be Profitable...

Even if you have only one gemcutting machine, whether for faceting or for cabbing, you can make money teaching.

There are many men and women who are fascinated with the craft of gemcutting...and they want to learn. Yes, people can teach themselves to cut gems but the learning process is so much faster and more certain when there's an "old pro" over the shoulder telling a student the how and why.

Lessons for faceting—a beginner's course generally runs about 25-35 hours—is priced anywhere from $100 to $500. Lessons for cabbing—a beginner's course generally runs about 10-15 hours— is priced from $100 to $300. The totals can run much higher, depending on length of course, hours of instruction time, and materials offered to the student for cutting.

Many gemcutting instructors get students from the local mineral or rock hound club. Others advertise. In Charlotte, NC, Henry

Underhill has been promoting and advertising faceting lessons for years and his Lapidary Arts business there fills up the classroom throughout the year. Here is the advertisement that Henry runs each month in *American Gemcutter Magazine,* official monthly publication of the American Society of Gemcutters:

> **A FUN PLACE** for you to be serious about
> learning to cut gems. 5-day course in faceting
> and cabbing. Equipment and supplies fur-
> nished. You keep what you cut. Cost:
> $375. 3019 Kilborne dr., Charlotte, NC 28205
> Phone 1-704-537-7099

Lapidary Arts provides a complete bank of Graves faceting and cabbing machines. A master promoter, Underhill often schedules in special faceting events and even gives each graduating student a free one-year membership in the American Society of Gemcutters. The Society sends the free bonus book to each student directly to Underhill and he hands out the book as part of the student package.

You don't necessarily need to gear up for a large student body per class as Lapidary Arts has done. But you can with a minimum of time, money and effort keep your gemcutting machines busy with paying students. Sit down and write up a short classified ad and then run it in the local paper.

> **FOR FUN OR PROFIT.** Learn gem-
> cutting. Equipment supplied. You keep the
> beautiful gems you cut. Classes starting now.
> For details, call   000-000-0000

You can use your own workshop as a classroom. Set the classes up two-three times a week. Evening hours are usually best. You can try it on weekends but most people are employed and want their weekends for other uses.

Do some hard thinking about what materials and instructions you'll use in your course. Remember, that you'll have to provide a beginner with everything...dopsticks, rough, adhesive, machine, laps, polishes, etc. Type up (or have typed) your own course materials and run off a small supply on a copying machine.

As a valuable promotional service to your new students, use some of the tuition money to buy them a one-year trial membership in the American Society of Gemcutters. The free book bonus program by ASG will provide each student with a nice gemcutting book and you can arrange with ASG to give out this bonus book as part of your curriculum package.

To get in contact with the Society, write to:

American Society of Gemcutters
Attn: Gerald Wykoff
PO Box 1991
York, PA 17405

Many retired people make a tidy extra income giving gemcutting lessons in their home. There are always some used machines on the market in case you wish to accommodate more than one student at a time. You'll find that a single instructor can usually handle about three students. When you get more than that, the fun goes out of teaching and the stress factor goes up a little, too.

Once you start giving faceting or cabbing lessons, contact one of the machine manufacturers. Many of them already have protected dealers but they'll usually be happy to work out some kind of discount arrangement for you should you wish to sell new machines to your students.

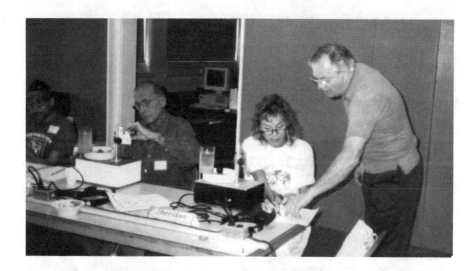

Teaching gemcutting can be a most pleasant and rewarding way to turn a profit from your gemcutting skills. Students are everywhere.

For obvious reasons, it generally doesn't pay to try and get one machine at discount on the promise that you intend to start teaching. When it comes right down to selling machines, most students take a few lessons to see if they like the craft. If they get bit by the gemcutting bug, chances are they'll soon be in the market for a machine.

The art of gemcutting is a valuable craft and any practioner with average skills can easily turn teaching into a profit maker.

Setting Up a Selling Plan...

All it takes to sell gemstones is an effective selling plan and some follow through. Why is it so easy? It's easy because people really want gems...and they're delighted if they get a bit extra for their money.

Selling gemstones properly therefore represents more of a consulting task than the customary sales pitch type selling. Too many gemcutters are realizing a substantial income from their marketing efforts to come to any other conclusion—many of them are anything but the traditional glib salesman type.

In becoming a supplier of gemstones to jewelers, good product and service will usually result in referrals to other jewelers who have intermittent needs for acquiring well cut stones. Regardless of the sales target, an attractive display of your gems goes a long way toward consummating the sale.

Don't underestimate the power of ordinary classified advertisements to advance your gemstone selling program. They're inexpensive—and they produce results almost without fail. Just keep in mind that all the planning in the world won't sustain success if there isn't excellence in the workshop. Here's where your best working talent should be expended...to cut the best stones possible.

Summary of Market Needs...

In summary, as a skilled gemcutter you have a wide variety of strategies for making money. With each of these marketing options, you undertake an obligation to accommodate their individualized needs. Let's quickly review the different markets.

The important rule to remember when developing a target market is that you will need to conform to the specialized needs of that market...and not all sales outlets are attracted to loose, unmounted gemstones.

A jewelry store or repair shop is an obvious and excellent target for selling cut gemstones.

These merchants are in the business, they have their own overhead, and they know the rules and pricing. They are determined to buy from you at a price low enough to ensure a profitable markup. That means you will probably realize the lowest stone price from this natural target. On the up side, jewelry stores and repair shops represent a continuing, long term business opportunity that takes little more

The spread of a convention floor can be quite impressive, but even more impressive is the heavy flow of traffic past your booth.

than an introduction of yourself and your work.

Altrnatively, a specialty or gift store can move jewelry items rather quickly and consequently their owners are often reluctant to take on loose, unmounted stones. They want finished jewelry items mostly, and as retailers they also want the lowest price available. Remember that many salesman will be calling on them so the competition will be more withering than with jewelry stores. If you're able to develop a jewelry line, this market can be lucrative. The type of jewelry, too, doesn't need to conform so much to the jeweler's traditional demands. Many cab cutters have found their sales curve and profits increasing when they began fashioning cabochons with attractive paper and plastic mountings.

Many profit seeking gemcutters try their business luck in the flea market arena...and some not-so-surprising successes have resulted. It's a bit different but it can be effective. Here, as with yard and garage sales, you are your own retailer.

With flea markets, it's strictly put out your wares on a table top and allow the prospective buyers to stop by and take a look.

A kiosk or vanilla box poses the same opportunities and the

same challenge. Loose, unmounted stone sales are very chancey but if you can come up with some pieces of jewelry the rewards can be considerable.

As you know, direct selling carries the greatest psychological or emotional risk but it can also be the most lucrative. And prospecting is a major key.Convention selling offers a good test for top quality and inexpensive lapidary items. To obtain a booth, just call the convention manager of the organization who can also provide you with details.

Convention sales are usually cash sales but because many convention goers are business people you probably should be prepared to work with credit cards. **Note:** As hinted at earlier, make sure cash sales are allowed on the convention floor. Many conventions are sponsored by tax-exempt organizations and the IRS frowns on cash or merchandise sale by exhibitors.

For the occasional gemstone sale you might not need a formal accounting setup, but you certainly need one if you have a serious and substantial marketing plan in mind. Keeping good records is a must.

A a final suggestion, an inexpensive personal computer—with all their marvelous accounting software packages—will help keep your business, inventory, and finances in good order. They're worth the investment.

Gem Sellers Must Disclose Treatment, Enhancement

It isn't unusual for any gemcutter to want to realize some profit from his craft. The output of a gemcutter is invariably valuable, even when the cutting is somewhat less than professional.

Still, in making preparations for any gemstone marketing program, first things come first.

The critical first thing in looking at retail dealers or final consumer is this: before commencing with any gemstone sales, you will need to make some gemological preparations. Those preparations include boning up on gemstone treatment and enhancement. Disclosure is more than just a word in the jewelry industry these days.

You can get into serious legal difficulties if you sell a

Treating and enhancing gemstones—to make them more durable and beautiful—is an industry all by itself in modern times. You must be familiar.

stone that has been significantly enhanced or treated and you don't disclose this information. For that reason, it's best that you study the manuals and find out what stones are treated and how. By having this knowledge available for your customers, you avoid the danger of inadvertently making a fraudulent sale.

To some extent, the public is aware that gems are often given a cosmetic treatment to produce a more beautiful gem. At the same time, it's obvious the public isn't aware of all the types of enhancement and treatment techniques. They just can't keep up with the rapidly developing methods used to promote the value of a gem by disguising or camouflaging its true value.

For this reason, the Federal Trade Commission has concerned itself about gem treatment and how the subject is handled with an unknowing public. In 1957, the FTC, supported by the Jewelers' Vigilance Committee, told the jewelry industry it had better inform the consumer of gem enhancement. Disclosure is one of the major

---

BLUE TOPAZ

Historically, only a few Blue Topaz have been found in nature. Now with the advent of modern technology, a process of irradiation has made it possible to change the color of certain types of Topaz to lovely shades of sky blue, thus making Blue Topaz one of the most popular stones today. Topaz is found mainly in Brazil, Nigeria, and Sri Lanka.

To maintain the brilliance of this beautiful gemstone, it should be immersed in a jewelry cleaner or in lukewarm soapy water and cleaned with a small bristle brush. From time to time, it is advisable to have our jeweler check the setting and clean the stone professionally. As with all gemstones, care should be taken to protect it from scratches and sharp blows.

A series of cards like the one above, intended for distribution to jewelry customers, were developed but they enjoyed little support or use by retailers.

---

topics of concern in the jewelry industry. This is where a professional gemcutter with good gemological knowledge can do the industry—and the buying public— a valuable service.

When the FTC first proposed disclosure obligations, the response wasn't all that great. Most jewelers didn't want to get into the disclosure thing. They claimed all the technical discussion would confuse buyers—and everyone knows that confused buyers do. They don't is what they do. Responding to the inaction, in the late 1980s a determined effort was made to fashion guidelines for disclosure of gem treatment. This effort resulted in the "Jewelry Industry Guide For Natural Gemstones, Synthetic Stones, and Imitation Stones."

Initially, the guidelines were developed as a joint effort by the American Gem Society, American Gem Trade Association, Jewelers of America, Jewelers Vigilance Committee and the Manufacturing Jewelers and Silversmiths of America. The heart of the new procedure consists of a series of easy to understand letter designations which are provided to gemstone buyers so the latter will be informed of different gemstone treatments before purchase.

Cutters Conform...

As a gemcutter you should be aware of these requirements, particularly if you engage in any gem treatments or enhancement methods yourself. Even if you don't personally carry out gem treatments, you should be aware that much of the rough you routinely buy is treated. This treatment should be disclosed to you, but often isn't. As one who sells to the public or the trade, you are still responsible for disclosing and the failure of your supplier to disclose to you doesn't relieve you of the your own responsibility.

The guidelines are aimed at two major goals.

First the designation guide is intended to provide communications language strictly for jewelry industry use, between wholesale dealers and cutters or between wholesale dealers, cutters and dealers.

Second, the guidelines show a united effort by the industry to respond to the need for more consumer information.

To conform properly to the system, every stone paper, memorandum, stone paper and tag should contain one or more of the short hand letter designations.

All gemstones are divided into three major grouping. These are:

"A" Designation

An "A" designates a gemstone that isn't normally treated or enhanced (garnet, peridot, etc.) and treated so rarely that any other designation would tend to be misleading.

"E" Designation

An "E" designates a stone that is normally treated (topaz, ruby, sapphire, aquamarine, etc.) and the type of treatment(s) is described with other letter designations.

Note: The "E" alone would designate only the typical type of treatment for a gem type: it could mean heat treatment for aqua but mean oiling for emerald. If you wish, you can replace the "E" with the proper letter code *e.g.*, "H" for aqua. If a stone is normally treated in some process but you can't provide definitively that it has received such treatment, you should assume it has been treated and mark the stone as an "E."

"N" Designation

If a stone has received no treatment and you can prove it, the stone may be marked with an "N." Documentation must accompany any stone to support the "N" designation.

Some future changes will be made to the enhancement guideline, but gemcutters should become familiar with the system of major elements that is described on the following three pages.

Not just consumers get burned buying treated stones that were undisclosed. A surprising number of gemcutters admit that they've bought both cut stones and rough they thought were natural but in fact had been treated. It's not too surprising then that most people in the jewelry and lapidary trade admit that consumers certainly should be told something of industry stone cosmetic practices. The problem today is that too many differences remain on how much, how and what should be disclosed. People who become confused don't buy and a fine line exists between intelligent disclosure and obfuscation through technical jargon.

Even in the early 1990s, the controversy of disclosure

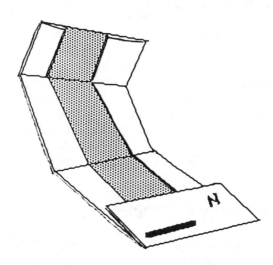

The majority of today's gemstones are routinely treated or enhanced. As a gemcutter, you really need to be familiar with all treatment processes..

and how to perform it properly was the burning subject of most jewelry organizations. Many industry people felt with some justification that the U. S. Federal Trade Commission "Guides for the Jewelry Industry" were insufficient.

Others support whole heartedly the new wording of the Guide:

"It is an unfair trade practice to sell or offer for sale any gem stone which has been enhanced by coating; application of colorless or colored oil; irradiation; surface diffusion; dyeing; heating; by the use of nuclear bombardment; or by any other means, without providing a description which informs the purchaser that said gemstone has been or may have been enhanced; and disclosure that a change in color or tinting is not permanent if such is the fact."

As a gemcutter wanting to sell your work, you would probably be well advised to disclose what you know about any stone and it's probable treatment—by you or by anyone else. Any changes in the industry guides are likely to be in wording with little change expected in substance. Some of the recommended disclosures are admittedly too long (they'll confuse people) and probably will be shortened. Basically the guides are here to stay for now and for the foreseeable future—or at least until some inventor comes along with a new treatment or enhancing process that must be dealt with.

What follows in the next few pages is a summary of most known gem treatment and enhancement procedures. Read over this list a few times until you're fairly conversant with all of the information and gem types. Your knowledge of these industry practices could mean the difference between a profitable sale and some uncomfortable time in a courtroom.

Your Responsibility to Disclose...

In the final analysis, it has become your responsibility to disclose any enhancement or treatment processes regardless of the type of buyer. You must even disclose to the jeweler—and especially to consumers. Of course the vendor who sold you rough or cut stones must have likewise disclosed to you—or marked the letter designation on any stone papers. In the absence of disclosure to you, you are still not relieved of your own responsibility to disclose.

**Jewelry Industry Guide
for
Natural Gemstone
Synthetic Stones
and
Imitation Stones**

PURPOSE

The purpose of the guidelines is to provide jewelry buyers—both consumers and trade—with vital descriptions of treatment and/or enhancement conduct on gemstones. Each stone will be assigned at least one letter with the likelihood of more letter designations if needed to identify additional processes. The coding system is to be used by manufacturers, gemcutters, wholesale suppliers, and retailers.

GLOSSARY

ENHANCEMENT: This is any process other than cutting and polishing which improves the appearance (color/clarity), durability, or availability of a gem).

NATURAL GEMSTONE

B   Bleaching: The use of chemicals or other agents to lighten or remove a gemstone's color

C   Coating: The use of such methods as lacquering, enameling, inking, foiling, or sputtering of film to improve appearance *i.e.*, provide color or add other special effects.

D   Dyeing: The introduction of coloring matter into a gemstone to give it new color, intensify present color or improve color uniformity.

F   Filling: The masking of surface cavities or fractures usual ly with glass or plastic, or another foreign sub stance to improve appearance.

I   Impregnation: General infusion of a substance such as paraffin or wax into a porous material.

L   Lasering: The use of a laser and chemicals to reach and al ter objectionable inclusions in diamonds.

O   *Oiling:*   The penetration of colorless oil (notice that this definition avoids colored oils such as are some times used with emerald) into voids and faults to improve overall appearance.

P   *Stabilization:*   The use of a colorless bonding agent (com- monly plastic) within a gemstone to improve dur ability and appearance.

R   *Irradiation:*   The use of a high energy or subatomic par- ticlebombardment to alter and improve a gem stone's color. Heating process often follows.

U   *Surface Diffusion:*   The use of high temperature and chemi cals resulting in the shallow penetration of color and/or asterism on and just below the surface of a gemstone.

IMITATION
AND
ASSEMBLED STONES

SYNTHETIC STONES
SYN: A laboratory grown stone that exhibits essentially the same physical, optical and chemical properties as its naturally occurring

counterpart *e.g.*, (the name of the material must always be used) synthetic emerald, synthetic ruby, etc.) The word "synthetic" cannot be used as a noun.

A SYN coded stone requires only normal care.

IMITATION STONES

IMIT: Laboratory grow material, that is used to simulate the appearance, but not necessarily duplicate the properties of the natural gemstone it imitates *e.g.*, synthetic cubic zirconia, synthetic sapphire, etc.

This designation also includes GGG, YAG, strontium titanate and other imitation gem materials. Except for strontium titanate, these stones generally require normal care.

ASSEMBLED STONES

ASBL: Multiple layers or combinations of manufactured and/or natural materials fused, bonded, or otherwise joined together to imitate the appearance of a naturally occurring gemstone, create a unique design or generate unusual color combinations.

ASSEMBLED STONE EXAMPLES

Opal: doublets, triplets
Garnet: glass doublets
Sapphire: synthetic sapphire doublets
Colorless Beryl: green bonding, and doublets
Reconstructed: turquoise, lapis lazuli

THESE STONES ARE NOT TREATED SO DISCLOSURE IS NOT AN ISSUE

Alexandrite
Andalusite
Apatite
Benitoite
Charoite
Chrysoberyl
(alexandrites or cat's eyes)
Feldspars
(some spectrolite, labradorite
and sunstone)
Garnet
(all varieties)
Hematite
Iolite
Rhodochrosite
Rhodonite
Sodalite
Spinel
Sugilite

Key to Listing
Colors:
B=black
Bl=blue
Br=brown
P=pink
R=red
W=white
G=green
P=purple
L=lavender

Y=yellow
O=orange
G=gold

Marketplace Presence
Amount of material in the market
Low=up to $1/3$
Medium=$1/3$ to $2/3$
High=$2/3$ or higher

Identification Clues
10x=10 power magnification

LISTING OF
TREATMENT PROCESSES
FOR NATURAL STONES

Amber

Treatment/Enhancement Techniques: Natural
Colors: Y-O-O/P
Procedure Used: Air oxidation
Expected Consequences: will probably darken with age
Permanence of Treatment: stable
Identification Clues: 10x—natural inclusions
Presence in Marketplace: high

Treatment/Enhancement Techniques: dyeing
Colors: Y-O-O/P-G
Procedure Used: organic dyes, sometimes analine dyes
Results Derived: sunlight may cause colors to fade
Permanence of Treatment: semi-stable to unstable
Identification Clues: 10x—color concentrations
Presence in Marketplace: medium

Amber

Treatment/Enhancement Techniques: heated oil
Colors: —
Procedure Used: linseed oil soak, sometimes in vacuum
Results Derived: inclusions are clarified
Permanence of Treatment: permanent
Identification Clues: 10x—"spangled" inclusions
Presence in Marketplace: high

Treatment/Enhancement Techniques: reconstituted
Colors: —
Procedure Used: heat/pressure
Results Derived: material slightly darkened as random pieces fused
Permanence of Treatment: variable
Identification Clues: 10x—elongated bubbles, sometimes seems
Presence in Marketplace: medium

Aquamarine

Treatment/Enhancement Techniques: natural
Colors: lt.-med. Bl
Procedure Used: natural beryl is rare in deep colors, greenish
Results Derived: low heat sometimes removes green color
Permanence of Treatment: permanent
Identification Clues: standard ident.
Presence in Marketplace: high

Emerald

Treatment/Enhancement Techniques: natural
Colors: G
Procedure Used: untreated emeralds are very rare
Results Derived: often highly included
Permanence of Treatment: variable
Identification Clues: high relief (internal and external) inclusions
Presence in Marketplace: low

Emerald

Treatment/Enhancement Techniques: oiled
Colors: G
Procedure Used: oil (cedar wood, Canadian balsam) filled cracks
Results Derived: clarity appearance improved (dye in oil regarded as unethical)
Permanence of Treatment: variables, can be dislodged/removed
Identification Clues: 10x—trapped air bubbles, low-relief inclusions
Presence in Marketplace: high

Treatment/Enhancement Techniques: impregnation
Colors: G
Procedure Used: resins filled crack (Example: Yehuda process)
Results Derived: helps durability, improves clarity appearance
Permanence of Treatment: relatively stable
Identification Clues: "color flash," low-relief inclusions, bubbles
Presence in Marketplace: medium (and growing)

Green Beryl

Treatment/Enhancement Techniques: natural
Colors: lt. G
Procedure Used:
Results Derived:
Permanence of Treatment: stable
Identification Clues: standard ident.
Presence in Marketplace: medium

Treatment/Enhancement Techniques: heated
Colors: lt. G
Procedure Used: controlled furnace temperature
Results Derived: turns gem aqua blue or modified green
Permanence of Treatment: permanent
Identification Clues: none
Presence in Marketplace: high

Green Beryl
Treatment/Enhancement Techniques: dyeing
Colors: drk G (emerald appearance)
Procedure Used: filling inclusions with dyed materials (probably
                unethical since results are same as dyed emerald)
Results Derived: simulates emerald
Permanence of Treatment: unstable
Identification Clues: 10x—dye peels from surface, dye
                concentrations (especially in blemishes)
Presence in Marketplace: low

Morganite
Treatment/Enhancement Techniques: natural
Colors: P-Y/P
Procedure Used:
Results Derived:
Permanence of Treatment: stable
Identification Clues: standard ident.
Presence in Marketplace: high

Treatment/Enhancement Techniques: heated
Colors: P
Procedure Used: controlled furnace temperature
Results Derived: improves pink hue (removes yellow)
Permanence of Treatment: permanent
Identification Clues: none
Presence in Marketplace: medium

Treatment/Enhancement Techniques: irradiation
Colors: P
Procedure Used: gamma fay, linear accelerator
Results Derived: improves pink hue
Permanence of Treatment: permanent
Identification Clues: none medium
Presence in Marketplace: medium

Golden Beryl

Treatment/Enhancement Techniques: natural
Colors: Y/G
Procedure Used:
Results Derived:
Permanence of Treatment: permanent
Identification Clues: standard ident.
Presence in Marketplace: low

Treatment/Enhancement Techniques: irradiation
Colors: Y-G-Y/G
Procedure Used: gamma ray, linear accelerator
Results Derived: deeps yellow, produces "Heliodor" variety
Permanence of Treatment: permanent
Identification Clues: none
Presence in Marketplace: high

Coral

Treatment/Enhancement Techniques: dyed
Colors: R-P
Procedure Used: analine dyes
Results Derived: enhance natural red, pin, black hues
Permanence of Treatment: stable
Identification Clues: remove dye with cotton swam
Presence in Marketplace: high

Treatment/Enhancement Techniques: bleach
Colors: G
Procedure Used: peroxide solution
Results Derived: turn black to golden
Permanence of Treatment: permanent
Identification Clues: bleaching induces smooth surface
Presence in Marketplace: high

Corundum

Treatment/Enhancement Techniques: ruby—glass fill
Colors: R-R/B-R/P
Procedure Used: molten glass filling cavities
Results Derived: improves perceived clarity by sealing voids
Permanence of Treatment: stable
Identification Clues: 10x—bubbles in the glass
Presence in Marketplace: low

Treatment/Enhancement Techniques: rubies—heat
Colors: R
Procedure Used: controlled furnace temperature
Results Derived: dissolves silk, cloudiness; improves red hue
Permanence of Treatment: permanent
Identification Clues: 10x—natural inclusions remain
Presence in Marketplace: low

Treatment/Enhancement Techniques: rubies—diffusion
Colors: R
Procedure Used: coated with chemical oxides and then heated
Results Derived: changes or enhances color
Permanence of Treatment: stable
Identification Clues: color concentrates on facet edges
Presence in Marketplace: low

Treatment/Enhancement Techniques: sapphire—heated
Colors: Bl
Procedure Used: controlled furnace temperature
Results Derived: darks or lightens hue; improves clarity
Permanence of Treatment: stable
Identification Clues: fractures, divots, silk partially dissolved
Presence in Marketplace: medium

Corundum

Treatment/Enhancement Techniques: sapphire—diffused
Colors: Bl
Procedure Used: coated with chemical oxides then heated
Results Derived: enhances and/or changes color
Permanence of Treatment: stable
Identification Clues: color
Presence in Marketplace: medium

Treatment/Enhancement Techniques: star—heated
Colors: R-Bl
Procedure Used: controlled furnace temperature
Results Derived: dissolves or reconfigures silk inclusions
                  depending on temperature used
Permanence of Treatment: stable
Identification Clues: 10x—irregularities in silk
Presence in Marketplace: medium

Treatment/Enhancement Techniques: yellow sapphire—heated
Colors: Y-O
Procedure Used: controlled furnace temperatures
Results Derived: enhances yellow, change yellow to orange hue
Permanence of Treatment: stable
Identification Clues: sometimes heat fractures
Presence in Marketplace: high

Treatment/Enhancement Techniques: yellow sapphire—
          irradiation:
Colors: Y/O
Procedure Used: gamma ray exposure
Results Derived: bright yellow, tends to fade
Permanence of Treatment: unstable
Identification Clues: light or heat removes color
Presence in Marketplace: low

Diamond

Treatment/Enhancement Techniques: irradiation
Colors: Y-O-B-B-G-M
Procedure Used: cyclotron, linear accelerator, gamma ray
Results Derived: produces thin, uniform color coating
Permanence of Treatment: stable
Identification Clues: some radiation stains, spectroscope, unusual
                             color not seen in natural colored diamond
Presence in Marketplace: medium

Treatment/Enhancement Techniques: heated
Colors: Y
Procedure Used: controlled furnace temperature
Results Derived: modifies natural yellow or irradiated colors
Permanence of Treatment: stable
Identification Clues: none
Presence in Marketplace: low

Treatment/Enhancement Techniques: fracture fill
Colors: —
Procedure Used: fill surface cracks
Results Derived: improves clarity appearance
Permanence of Treatment: stable
Identification Clues: blue "flash;" high- and low-relief inclusions
Presence in Marketplace: high

Treatment/Enhancement Techniques: laser drill-bleach
Colors: W
Procedure Used: drill into inclusion, sometimes fill with bleach
Results Derived: improves clarity appearance
Permanence of Treatment: stable
Identification Clues: 10x— high-relief tunnels visible
Presence in Marketplace: high

Diamond

Treatment/Enhancement Techniques: coating
Colors: B-G-R-Y
Procedure Used: clear coatings on pavilion
Results Derived: changes, improves color
Permanence of Treatment: unstable
Identification Clues: often peels, 10x-edges visible
Presence in Marketplace: low

Ivory

Treatment/Enhancement Techniques: dyed
Colors: W
Procedure Used: tea soak, shoe polish or dye, including analine dye
Results Derived: gives antiqued appearance
Permanence of Treatment: unstable
Identification Clues: 10x—color concentrations, unnatural hue
Presence in Marketplace: medium

Treatment/Enhancement Techniques: bleached
Colors: W
Procedure Used: soak in peroxide solution
Results Derived: removes, lightens natural color
Permanence of Treatment: variable
Identification Clues: none
Presence in Marketplace: high

Treatment/Enhancement Techniques: heated
Colors: W
Procedure Used: controlled furnace temperature
Results Derived: "antiques" or darkens natural hue
Permanence of Treatment: variable
Identification Clues: 10x—burned areas, no dye concentrations
Presence in Marketplace: low

Jadeite

Treatment/Enhancement Techniques: dyed
Colors: W-G-Y-G-Bl-B-L
Procedure Used: analine dye in pores
Results Derived: adds, changes, enhances color (some alcohol based Hong Kong dyes very unstable—test with treated cotton swab)
Permanence of Treatment: variable
Identification Clues: 10x—dye concentrations
Presence in Marketplace: high

Treatment/Enhancement Techniques: irradiation
Colors: L
Procedure Used: gamma ray exposure
Results Derived: turns some jadeites to lavender
Permanence of Treatment: variable
Identification Clues: none
Presence in Marketplace: low

Lapis Lazuli

Treatment/Enhancement Techniques: dyed
Colors: B
Procedure Used: soak in analine dye
Results Derived: improves or changes color (dying is often done with sodalite to produce imitation lapis)
Permanence of Treatment: unstable
Identification Clues: 10x—dye concentrations; test/remove with acetone treated cotton swab
Presence in Marketplace: high

Opal

Treatment/Enhancement Techniques: smoked
Colors: multi-colored, including black
Procedure Used: carbon smoke impregnation
Results Derived: gives black opal appearance
Permanence of Treatment: unstable
Identification Clues: carbon concentrations, especially on edges
Presence in Marketplace: low

Opal

Treatment/Enhancement Techniques: dyed
Colors: B
Procedure Used: soak in silver nitrate, or soak in sugar and carbonize in sulphuric acid
Results Derived: gives boulder opal appearance of black opal
Permanence of Treatment: unstable
Identification Clues: 10x—color concentration, unnatural appearance
Presence in Marketplace: low

Treatment/Enhancement Techniques: impregnation
Colors: —
Procedure Used: oil, wax or plastic with pressure, vacuum
Results Derived: improves play of color
Permanence of Treatment: unstable
Identification Clues: hot point (dangerous!), acetone treated cotton swab, sophisticated instruments sometimes necessary
Presence in Marketplace: medium

Pearl

Treatment/Enhancement Techniques: bleached
Colors: W
Procedure Used: soak in peroxide solution (this is generally regarded as standard pearl manufacturing process)
Results Derived: lightens hue or dark blemishes
Permanence of Treatment: stable
Identification Clues: none

Treatment/Enhancement Techniques: coating/dyeing
Colors: W-P-G
Procedure Used: soak in organic dyes (sometimes analine dyes)
Results Derived: modify and improve color, hide blemishes
Permanence of Treatment: variable
Identification Clues: 10x—dye concentrations
Presence in Marketplace: medium

Pearl
Treatment/Enhancement Techniques: irradiation
Colors: Bl-P-B-R
Procedure Used: gamma ray exposure
Results Derived: produces blue, gray, magenta hues
Permanence of Treatment: permanent
Identification Clues: laboratory needed to detect darker nucleus
Presence in Marketplace: low

Quartz
Treatment/Enhancement Techniques: amethyst—heated
Colors: Y-G-P-B
Procedure Used: controlled furnace temperature
Results Derived: yields amethyst, citrine, Smokey quartz hues
Permanence of Treatment: permanent
Identification Clues: none
Presence in Marketplace: high

Treatment/Enhancement Techniques: chalcedony—dyed
Colors: R-O-Y-B-Br-G
Procedure Used: analine and other dyes, muriatic acid, heat
Results Derived: produces multi-colored results
Permanence of Treatment: stable
Identification Clues: color concentrations
Presence in Marketplace: high

Treatment/Enhancement Techniques: citrine—heated
Colors: Y-Y/R
Procedure Used: controlled furnace temperature
Results Derived: gives orange-reddish cast to yellow quartz

Permanence of Treatment: permanent
Identification Clues: usually reddish cast is visible
Presence in Marketplace: high

Quartz

Treatment/Enhancement Techniques: rock crystal—quench
cracking   **Colors:** multi colors
Procedure Used: heating then cooling rapidly (in water)
Results Derived: maze of cracks that accept dyes
Permanence of Treatment: unstable
Identification Clues: dye concentrations in cracks
Presence in Marketplace: medium

Treatment/Enhancement Techniques: rock crystal—dyed
Colors: R-G
Procedure Used: in conjunction with quench cracking
Results Derived: variety of colors, usually red and green
Permanence of Treatment: permanent
Identification Clues: dye concentrations in cracks, pores
Presence in Marketplace: medium

Treatment/Enhancement Techniques: rock crystal—irradiation
Colors: multi colors
Procedure Used: gamma ray exposure
Results Derived: yields multi colors, amethyst, ametrine
Permanence of Treatment: stable
Identification Clues: none
Presence in Marketplace: high

Topaz

Treatment/Enhancement Techniques: colorless—irradiation
Colors: Bl-Br
Procedure Used: gamma ray exposure, linear accelerator, neutron-
irradiated
Results Derived: yields yellow brown and (rarely) blue*
Permanence of Treatment: stable
Identification Clues: none
Presence in Marketplace: high

Topaz

Treatment/Enhancement Techniques: colorless—heated*
Colors: Bl-P
Procedure Used: controlled furnace temperature
Results Derived: yields varying blue and pink hues
Permanence of Treatment: stable
Identification Clues: unnatural vivid blue colors
Presence in Marketplace: high
    *irradiation is intermediate step in producing blue topaz:
irradiated topaz is subsequently heated to produce the blue variety

Treatment/Enhancement Techniques: brown/yellow—heated
Colors: Bl-P
Procedure Used: controlled furnace temperature
Results Derived: turns irradiated brown topaz blue or pink
Permanence of Treatment: stable
Identification Clues: none
Presence in Marketplace: high

Tourmaline

Treatment/Enhancement Techniques: indicolite—heated
Colors: lt. Bl, multi colors
Procedure Used: Controlled furnace temperature
Results Derived: reduces blue hue, changes blue to green or
                greenish blue
Permanence of Treatment: stable
Identification Clues: none
Presence in Marketplace: high

Treatment/Enhancement Techniques: rubellite—irradiation
Colors: P-R
Procedure Used: gamna ray exposure, linear accelerator
Results Derived: deepens red, darkens pink
Permanence of Treatment: stable
Identification Clues: none
Presence in Marketplace: high

Tourmaline
Treatment/Enhancement Techniques: pale—irradiation
Colors: Br
Procedure Used: gamma ray exposure
Results Derived: changes to green, or changes yellow to brown
Permanence of Treatment: stable
Identification Clues: none
Presence in Marketplace: high

Turquoise
(rarely unenhanced or treated in some way)
Treatment/Enhancement Techniques: dyed/coating
Colors: Bl
Procedure Used: liquid black shoe polish effective
Results Derived:
Permanence of Treatment: variable
Identification Clues: 10x—coating is visible, especially in pores
Presence in Marketplace: medium

Treatment/Enhancement Techniques: impregnation
Colors: Bl
Procedure Used: wax, plastic, paraffin and sometimes oils
Results Derived: improves color and workability, sometimes
                    improves durability
Permanence of Treatment: variable
Identification Clues: hot point (dangerous!), 10x—impregnating
                    materials often visible under magnification
Presence in Marketplace: high

Treatment/Enhancement Techniques: reconstitution
Colors: Bl
Procedure Used: combined with plastic coating
Results Derived: unites loose turquoise, deepens color and makes it
                    more uniform
Permanence of Treatment: variable
Identification Clues: 10-x—texture revealing of process, hot point
                    (dangerous!)
Presence in Marketplace: high

Howlite
Treatment/Enhancement Techniques: dyed
Colors: turquoise Bl
Procedure Used: blue dye (often analine) in howlite imitate
                    turquoise very closely)
Results Derived: yields multi colors, amethyst, ametrine
Permanence of Treatment: variable
Identification Clues: 10x—dye concentration, then standard
                    identification tests
Presence in Marketplace: low

Zircon
Treatment/Enhancement Techniques: heated
Colors: Y-Bl-R-Br
Procedure Used: controlled furnace temperatures
Results Derived: Variable but often turns browns to red, green,
                    yellow or blue
Permanence of Treatment: variable
Identification Clues: none
Presence in Marketplace: high

Zoisite
Treatment/Enhancemennt Techniques: heated
Colors: Bl-Bl/P
Procedure Used: controlled furnace temperature
Results Derived: changes brownish zoisite to blue/purple hue
Permanence of Treatment: stable
Identification Clues: none
Presence in Marketplace: high

Cutter Prepares
Release Form

Repairing gems can be a very lucrative business for gemcutters. If breakage, though, isn't carefully handled it can be a very disastrous business.

Philip Thompson of Springfield, MA, who specializes in faceting repairs, has an effective release form that he asks his clients to sign. Before Phil will accept a stone for repair the owner must sign the release form. The wording goes like this:

> In leaving your stone with us for whatever repair is agreed upon, you understand, accept, and fully agree to the following conditions...
>
> While in our possession, we will take all necessary precautions, and handle your gem in a professional manner at all times, to insure it's safety...
>
> However, in any gemstone, there may be inclusions, bubbles, fissures, cracks, and invisible pressures,which the heat and shock of cutting and polishing can cause to develop to the point where the stone can pit, chip, crack, fracture, split, and even explode into several pieces and in some cases, can cause a color change...
>
> While this rarely happens, should anything of this nature occur, we can not take any responsibility for any damage or loss of value to the stone whatsoever...
>
> Signature_____
> Date_____

How Much to Charge?
A Basis For Charging
For Your Work

The question of charging for your services can indeed be a perplexing one.

It was just as difficult for gemcutter R. C. McAllister, of Palm Bay, FL, but he worked out his own system.

R. C. questioned many of his colleagues on their approach, and Dr. Harold Smith of Chapel Hill, NC, came up with a solution that is fair regardless of the cut or material. Dr. Smith had attached a timer in the power line of his Ultra Tec drive and this device would accumulate the time that the machine motor ran. This allowed him to charge by the hour for the work, and the time charges were indisputably correct.

Not having the expertise to do this, R. C. decided that an equally fair method would be—regardless of cut or material—a

These Michael Dyber creations took time and talent. Pricing for the creative input is tough, but you must recoup for materials, time, and tools.

setup charge plus a carat charge.

As a result, R. C. charges $35 for setup plus $5 per carat or any fraction thereof for the finished stone. Example: finished stone weight is 10 carats

Set Up $35
Cutting $50 — $5 per carat—finished weight
                      regardless of the design cut
Total $85

In the event that an unsuitable material is presented for him to cut, or an unreasonable demand or request is made—the setup price goes up accordingly. This allows R. C. to discourage the cutting of the "junk" stones so many people "mine" in the roadside tourist traps. Once in a while a good stone is presented for cutting, but most is not much better than common driveway gravel.

R. C. says he finds that his rate actually figures out to be less per hour than the average pay for a car mechanic at the local garage. He feels strongly that any rate less than this is unfair to the cutter.

How To Figure Basic Charges...

How much should you charge for cutting?

It's a challenge that every good gemcutter faces sooner or later.

A number of approaches exist, but consistency is still the principle objective. This way, customers can predict their costs and you save a lot of explanation.

Cut is Criteria . . .

The rates for cutting stones depends on the type of cut to be used. The more complex the cut, the more time it takes, and thus, the higher the rate. The different cuts have been divided into three general groups for simplicity in pricing.

These groups and the general cuts that they contain are listed on page 89.

There are a number of additional charges involved in cutting a gem and these are relatively the same for all stone. A charge should

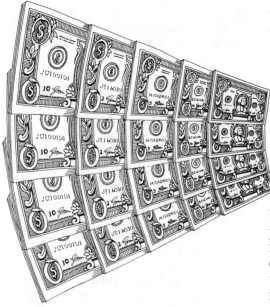

be included—in addition to the actual faceting—for such items as:

◆ rough orientation
◆ dopping
◆ initial shaping
◆ transferring
◆ undopping
◆ cleanup

These factors, plus the basic facet placement and polishing, account for the flat rate charge for the first carat of finished gemstone weight. Whether the finished stone weights 1/5 ct. or 1 ct. the charge is the same—the flat rate.

The larger the stone, the longer it takes to cut although the increased time per carat becomes less the larger the stone is. This is reflected in the rates by a charge of 5 cents per point ($5 per carat) for the 2nd, 3rd, and 4th carat of finished gemstone weight, and a charge of 3 cents per point ($3 per carat) for any weight over 4 carats.

As an example, the cutting fee for a 6.5 carat emerald cut gemstone would be figured as follows (because the emerald is a step cut it is in Group II):

1st ct @ flat rate	$25.00
next 3 ct @ 5¢/pt	$15.00
next 2.5 ct @ 3¢/pt	$ 7.50
	$ 47.50

The cost can also be found by using the graph shown to the right. By going to 5¼ ct on the bottom of the graph, then straight up to the Group I line, and then straight left to the total dollar cost scale.

Following are the grouping of cuts that R. C. follows:

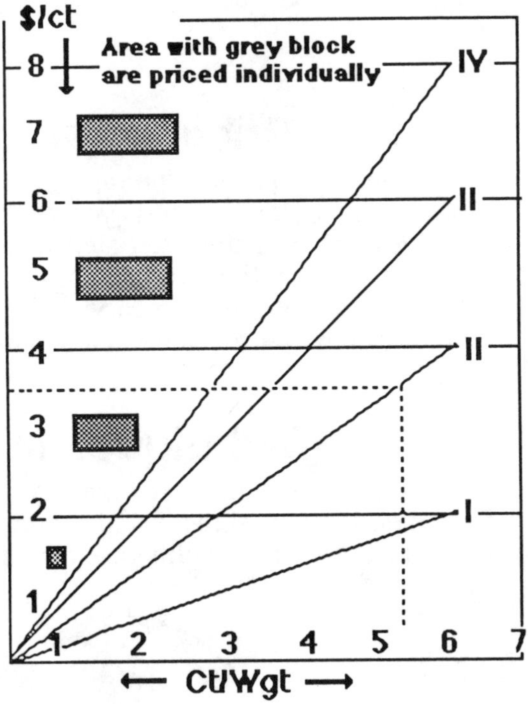

GROUP 1

The Standard Rounds: standard brilliant, Swiss cut, zircon cut, commercial cuts

GROUP 2

The step cuts: any shape Fancy round cuts: pin fire, double mirror brilliant

GROUP 3

Double brilliant cuts, Ultima Cuts, mixed cuts: any shape, Portuguese cut, Barion cut

As for recutting and stone repair work, in the late 80s R. C. was doing this at a bench rate of $15 per hour. Lately, professional gemcutters quote a minimum hourly rate of $25 per hour for any work.

Pricing Cabochons...

Cutting cabochons presents an even more difficult challenge if pricing by the carat. Unless you're dealing with opal, high quality lapis, expensive jadeite, asteriated stones or the like, the carat value often exerts less influence than does shape, appearance, and type of cabochon, faceted stone, or carved piece. The cut or carved stone is more important for its craft/talent content than for its carat content.

Techniques in Selling...

Many gemcutters seek non-traditional ways to realize a profit from their lapidary skills. Such a commendable objective is not only understandable but is well worth pursuing. After all, there aren't that

It's pretty difficult to turn away a professional gemcutter who places his stones carefully and attractively in a nice display case, then makes a professional presentation. Organization usually shows professionalism.

many skilled gemcutters in the world and the result of their work is highly desired. Given overseas competition anymore, a new approach is often the salvation for a profit venture.

Surprisingly enough, though, many gemcutters go on year after year cutting magnificent, saleable stones. Yet these stones accumulate in the gemcutter's shop, unmounted and unsold...despite the fact that the gemcutter might dearly wish to exchange them for extra money.

If gemcutters can turn out beautiful work, and these stones are highly desirable why then are so many competent gemcutters still searching for a way to turn a small profit?

Most of the time, gemcutters fail to produce income from their talent simply because they don't go out and try to sell. The unbroken rule is: nothing happens until somebody sells something.

If there are that many gemcutters who want to sell beautiful gemstones and that many people who want to buy them, why are so many of these talented lapidaries still wondering where the magical element called profits exist? Why is it seemingly so difficult to make money when your talents are so valuable?

The answer isn't difficult to find.

These profit searching individuals simply don't understand— or avoid—the principles involved in making a profit.

Let's look at the basic rule of commerce, valid whether deep down you're a capitalist, a socialist, or some other economics type.

What separates the profit making gemcutters from those who only wish for some sort of income is this basic realization:

"Nothing happens until somebody sells something."

That's right! Commerce is impossible until goods and service

If you have an electro plating outfit, a good merchandising trick is to give gold jewelry items a quick 24K gold "flash plate." Items look new.

get exchanged. Somebody has something that someone else needs or wants. Often as not, money is the element that enables people to carry out these vital exchanges. If money is the tool, selling is the process for this ageless propensity among human beings to truck, sell and barter their talents.

That's why the selling principle above might sound overly simplistic and obvious. It is both of these things all right. Yet it's also the heart and soul of commerce...and you would be astonished at the number of people who don't seem to understand that you can't make money if you won't or can't sell your work. Daydreaming is not an acceptable response to human desire or need.

You simply must sell something if you expect to make money. How much to charge for your work, the quantity of goods, products, or services immediately available, how many people want a certain thing are all subordinate aspects of selling. These considerations will be worked out in the selling process itself. The sale is the vital issue.

Given the necessity for selling something, you should then understand a second rule of selling. That the product or service you sell may be a necessity or a luxury is primarily irrelevant. A gemstone needs only to satisfy a want. Therefore:

"The extent and skill of selling required is directly proportional to the perceived level of necessity."

If you are starving or thirsty, it takes precious little selling skill to convince you of the need for food or water. In most cases, the principle task of selling food and thirst quenching liquids merely involves making it available. The selling process in a modern supermarket is extremely subtle: selling is often limited to encouraging brand selection and any human or personal involvement often consists of checking out and paying. Likewise, when you stop for gasoline for your car, nowadays they don't even pump the gas for you. You do it yourself, and pay the cashier. In these cases, you are buying necessities and the sales skills have been largely directed at you beforehand through advertising.

Let's transfer the selling situation to a jewelry store, though. Yes, people come into a jewelry store to purchase in the same manner as they do in a grocery store or service station. That is, they have a predisposition to purchase. In a jewelry buying situation they generally aren't directing themselves at necessities—so the

complexity of a jewelry purchase often entails knowledgeable assistance. That's another way of saying that they require a goodly contribution of "salesmanship." No one needs to sell you on the merits of a quart of milk, a brand of bread, or a gallon of unleaded gasoline. The quality of a Tanzanite gemstone is another matter. The average buyer is incapable of ascertaining the value of such a gemstone purchase and would want expertise and salesmanship.

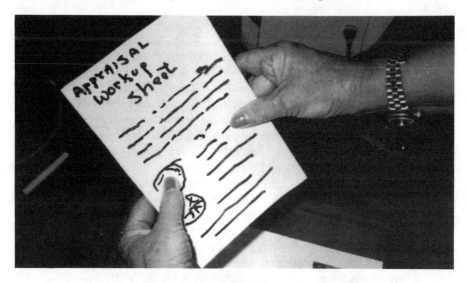

It's a good idea to get your stones appraised because certification is rapidly becoming the fifth "Big C" for determining gemstone value.

Admittedly, this is where many amateur and would-be professional gemcutters come up short. Some claim, "...well, I'm just not a salesman type," and others claim, "I hate salesmen (or saleswomen)!" Neither is an appropriate attitude for someone who would like to see some reward for their efforts and talent. Adhering to the first two basic laws of selling, only through selling will profits be made and only by the application of sales effort will someone buy. You aren't selling water in the desert where your only responsibility is to make the water available for someone who will pay obediently. You're selling a luxury item—and that requires salesmanship.

Gemcutters, however skilled, are no different from any other craftsman. If they ever expect to produce income from gemcutting either the gemcutter or somebody representing them will have to get out there in the mix-it-up world and exert selling effort.

All the wishing and all the profit potential represented by filled cases of loose, cut gemstones won't bring in one penny of income until that fundamental act is performed—sell something. Not surprisingly, many gemcutters find themselves unable to overcome the barrier of selling. The emotional cost is just too great.

Yet, the emotional reward is what gemcutters should seek. Of course, there is a possibility of a rejection. But there is the satisfaction also of watching the expression on a happy buyer's face, clutching a magnificent gemstone and imagining how it will look in the wearing. There are few objects in the world quite so beautiful as a well-cut gemstone and when you can bring this union of stone and buyer together, you have accomplished something that should provide you with a reward. Believe it or not, people actually like you for doing them this grand favor. This brings us to the third law of selling. This is:

"Many sales are made simply because the buyer likes and trusts the sales person. And this sense of trusting is often developed in the first few minutes."

People sometimes fail to understand this particle of human relations. People often buy something simply because they like the salesperson: they wish to reward good, effective sales effort. They can buy a beautiful stone in any jewelry store, repair shop, or from any gemcutter, but for a personal liking or appreciation they buy from YOU! Selling is part personality, but good work and appropriate pricing count, too.

It doesn't have to be based solely on personality and selling skill. When carried out properly, selling gemstones can be a smooth and almost pleasurable experience. A salesperson/gemcutter can make an informative and attentive pitch, the stone is just what the customer wants, the price seems about right so the deal is closed.

This minuet of enlightened selling can create positive feelings for both parties to the event, the buyer and the seller. It's not unusual for buyers to return long after to the person who sold them a stone or piece of jewelry and express continuing satisfaction with the purchase. These kinds of transactions are so fulfilling that a gemcutter should actively work to develop selling skills.

All too often these days the dancing skills of sales people that consumers encounter on the telephone, at the local mall or at the front door are declining. Walk into the average jewelry store and this observation will be confirmed. The gemological skills of some of the sales help is indeed appalling.

Recognizing the need for qualified sales people in jewelry, the Gemological Institute of America offers correspondence and resident training in gemology. Many of these GIA graduates move into the jewelry industry. Their presence is helpful. Despite the high quality of GIA's course materials, precious little training is given about gem cutting or even the attributes of cut stones. This is unfor-

The Gemological Insitute of America does a remarkable job in providing gem-ological—and sales—training. Consider the wisdom of taking some of these courses, even by mail correspondence if necessary.

tunate when the value of a gemstone often represents the major component in the price of a piece of jewelry. Little wonder then that Lawrence Chonko, marketing professor at Baylor University's Center for Professional Selling and Sales Management, estimates that three of 10 salespeople lack the basics of their trade.

If the sales person in the average jewelry store lacks the knowledge of the trade, h/she usually also is disinterested in developing a long-term interest and relationship with a customer. The resulting business fallout from the reluctance to encourage long-time and loyal customers can be considerable. Any business has a tough enough time succeeding. Why accelerate its chances to fail by under performance of the selling function's goal of customer retention?

A natural vacuum exists.

Into this vacuum an enterprising gemcutter can adkvance. To produce profits, s/he needs to master only a few fundamentals of selling:

   ✔ How to be pleasant, honest and memorable.
   ✔ How to discuss gemstones and their quality evaluation in non-technical   terms
   ✔ How to promote long-term customer relationships.

These techniques can be learned easily enough. For example, one gemcutter/salesman attacks the memorable idea by never leaving his house without his business cards. He even promises to pay anyone $100 if they catch him without a business card.

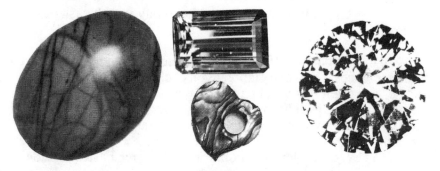

The nice thing about a lapidary business is that you can offer a whole, beautiful range of products...faceted stones, cabs, carvings, jewelry. Faceted stones, like it or not, return the best profit.

If he does someone a favor or a courtesy, he remembers to give them his business card. He engages people in conversations and then hands them his business card "...in case they ever need a gem stone."

Carefully reading the newspaper each day, he notes any announcement or favorable story about someone he knows and then clips it out and mails it to the person with a "I've Been Reading About You in the Newspapers" card. Of course, his own business card is also attached.

What is the selling process? It consists of three parts:

Opening   (Introduction)

Development   (Informative)

Closing   (Ask for the order)

You can read all the books and manuals you want about salesmanship but the three fundamentals above are what it's all about. You get into the sales presentation, show the benefits—and then ask the buyer to buy. In any sales situation you enter, make certain these three basics are covered and you will be assured that a complete sales effort has been made. It can be as simple as:

Opening—"Hello."
Development—"This blue topaz gold ring with diamond melee accent stones will look magnificent on your finger, and it costs only $172."
Closing—"Would you like to buy it with cash or on installment?"

That's right, an effective sales presentation can be as short as three sentences. You can elaborate on each of the elements, of course, and often this will be the best course of action. A more complicated piece of jewelry might require more of an explanation—and you will need to disclose the irradiation enhancement that makes the topaz blue.

As even simpler incorporation of the three basics includes a display of the same ring with a friendly sales tag that reads:

> ### John Jones Special
> 14K Gold Ring With 6.52/ct Swiss blue
> topaz and .55/ct TW white diamonds.
> Only $172.   Terms Available.

Selling Sequence...

The Opening is the easiest part. But it's the part that scares people most—and produces the most selling errors.

"How are you?" is generally considered the most ineffective, dumbest opening line a sales person can make. "Can I help you?" is a close second for total asininity.

Say most master salesman: be honest and forthright right up front. To open a sales presentation state your name, and offer a benefit "...a hexagonal shaped blue stone would look great with those geometric shaped ear rings you're wearing") or a testimonial opener ("Your name was given to me by..." . If you're really easy dealing and talking with people, use a "misdirected opener." A misdirected opener is a conversational technique that's intended to ease a prospect's initial defensive response to the sales person's approach.

For example, here is a misdirected opener to a woman who enters a jewelry store:

"Hello. I'm Jim Jones. The weather report says it's blistering hot out today but you don't seem to be showing any surrender to high temperature."

That kind of opener has nothing to do with jewelry or gemstones. It does, though, offer the woman an easy chance to exchange a pleasantry—and realize that she won't be getting involved with a hard pressure sales person. Remember: first impressions may not be the best impressions, but they do tend to remain.

Be wary of displaying too much of your technical knowledge, because you may confuse a prospective buyers with too much fact—and confused people seldom buy.

Once you've introduced yourself, start building rapport. Continue to talk about the customer's clothes, refrigerator magnet collection, anything other than the business at hand. Do you remember the last part of selling principle three? It states that trusting is usually developed in the first few minutes.

Be Ready to Transition...

Be natural and pleasant while you talk. Maintain eye contact (but don't stare them down!) and use the customer's name often.   Have a firm understanding of the transition point between the opening and the development phase. In the opening, you simply talk and listen.. Inexperienced sales people, think they have to do all the talking. That's simply not correct. Let the customer do most of the talking, especially during the opening. Find out—without interrogating—what you can. It's vital, of course, for you to know your gemstone thoroughly but first try —mentally—to fit any gemstone to your customer's wants and needs.

Once you transition into the development phase, begin to discuss what you've learned with your own knowledge. Involve the customer in your sales presentation by pointing out specific elements. "Did you know that the total reflectivity of a diamond is only 17 per cent of all the light that hits it? Interesting, isn't it?"

During the development is when the customer will usually start injecting or setting you up for a "no." There isn't much doubt in anyone's mind what "no" means. To an experienced salesman, though, "no" usually doesn't really mean "no." It means "I want more information" or "you haven't convinced me that I want or need that stone." That's right. "No" often refers to the customer's nagging concern or a request for additional information.

If the "no" is emphatic, it's not unusual for a seasoned sales person to respond, "I know how you feel. I felt the same way until I learned more about it." In other words, a no often means that your development is incomplete. It won't hurt to continue talking

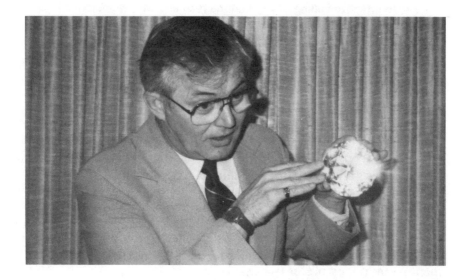

To develop your own selling skills, pay a visit to a good jewelry store and listen to the presentations made by trained salespeople. It's the best, cheapest sales training there is. Then practice, practice—in front of a mirror.

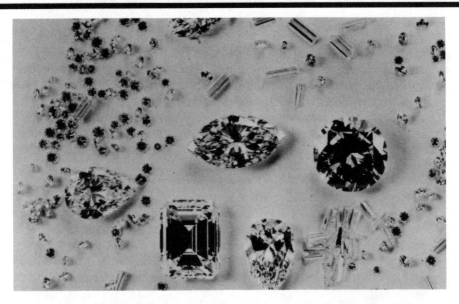

The key to effective selling of a gemstone is to allow the gemstones to sell themselves. Let the customer do most of the talking...and ask questions.

about the stone...or *misdirect*. Change the subject a bit, and then come back to the issue: the gemstone.

The Close...

The closing is when any salesman might choke a bit. This is where the element of refusal or rejection is involved. No one likes rejection. To avoid such a possibility, many salesman actually avoid closing. Naturally, they lose the sale, but they escape a potential emotional hit.

The true sales person carries the development right to the closing. It is an oddity, but many presentations fizzle out because the sales person doesn't even try to close the deal. Any one of a number of closing techniques could be used. Asking a prospect what payment method they prefer is a good closing test .

To make the closing even easier—and with less threat to your self-esteem or ego—get the customer to express their interest in a particular type of stone, cut, size, etc.

As a last, honest resort, simply ask the customer if they'd like to buy the proffered gemstone.

One Man's Clutter—
Another Man's Collectible...

When you're clearing out all the loose stones in your work shop, the gems you unearth are actually quite valuable for use both in jewelry or as collectables.

The word of advice is: don't overlook the value of any cut gemstone. Even that washed out amethyst for which you don't hold a particularly high regard is valuable to someone.

Remember the old adage: "One man's clutter is anotherman's collectible." Take a look at your treasures and ask yourself:

✔ Am I storing gemstones whose value is appreciating at a lower rate than the cost of the space they're occupying?

✔ Do I have that special cabochon, carving, or faceted stone in a storage box or envelope and I   really don't want to keep it all that

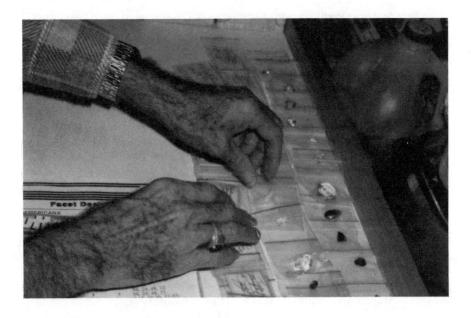

Every gemcutter who has been cutting for awhile can open up a case or drawer and probably find an excellent selection of well-cut, commercial quality stones with which to launch a stone selling business.

The Smithsonian Institution in Washington DC has one of the finest gem-stone collecitons in the world, and most of the gems were donated, enabling curators to swap gems for other, more desired gems.

much anymore?

Now is the time to unload them. If you're saving certain stores or if you've just put them in a box when you finished cutting them take a minute to evaluate them. Are they worth anything? Are you going to use them in the near or distant future? Can they be sold to someone?

Perhaps your children or relatives would want them. If that's the case, give them away to your loved ones. Most gemcutters do this anyway but you should live so long as to meet a gemcutter who still doesn't have a leftover surplus cache of gems.

Plus, don't overlook the tax advantage of giving away valuable gemstones to churches and charities. The tax deduction rules on donating gemstones and antiques depend on how long you owned the item, what the charity will do with the item, and the value of the donations you made. It's worth investigating.

Likewise, don't overlook the local museum. The value of gems you donate to a museum is still tax deductible. True, the IRS has lately cracked down on kited appraisals for gems donated to museums. It was an ugly, greedy game for awhile back in the 70s and 80s. That's when tax dodgers bought a parcel of low quality gems, obtained a "kited" appraisal of their value, and then donated the batch to the nearest museum. The dodge gave the donors enormous tax writeoff benefits...and it was a fraud on the public, pure and simple. That's when the IRS started knuckling down. No more tricks like that, the tax collectors said, and they started turning down the values. A legitimate donation of gems at their fair price, though, doesn't raise tax collectors' eyebrows

Not only are tax rules complicated,but they're also changing, so check with a tax accountant on the latest allowance.

For certain stones you may need the expertise of a certified appraiser. Sometimes museums, auction galleries and dealers will give you a fair appraisal. This only works to your advantage if the firm doing the appraisal is not going to be the buyer.

If you haven't had the items in your workshop professionally appraised within the past five years, call the American Society of Appraisers (800-ASA-VALU) to find a certified gem appraiser near you. The $100+ per hour fee that some appraiser charge is money well spent. Not only will you have verification for sales and for insurance purposes, but you'll have a good knowledge of what your gemstone inventory is worth.

The four "C's" (cut, carat, clarity, color) have long ruled as the fundamentals of gem sales, but the fifth "C"—for certification—is rapidly gaining prominence and acceptance.

In a pinch, refer to the Monthly Pricing Guide in *American Gemcutter Magazine,* official monthly publication of the American Society of Gemcutters. You have to be a member to get this publication but the $30 annual fees are well worth it. The Guide provides wholesale prices (what retail dealers pay for stones) on a one-carat basis. Price ranges are provided from low commercial to near investment grade colored stones and diamonds. You should use published price guides to help establish price-value in your gems but don't be a slave to the guides...they often provide you only with an averaged price for smaller stones. For most of your stones, you will need an appraised price or you will need to calculate an appropriate price, remembering that as carat size increases arithmetically the price goes up somewhat geometrically.

A word of advice should be sounded, though. The Guide prices are averaged approximations. They won't provide the precise value that a certified appraiser will give you.

Selling Your Gemstones...

Armed with your appraisal, you can sell confidently (today's consumer is so nervous about buying gemstones that s/he almost demands some kind of certificate be a part of the sale)—becausethe appraisal represents an educated estimate of what your asking price should be. You can prepare to sell your gems in several ways.

Put them in your garage sale. Be cautious with this wheel-and-deal approach because you don't want to sell the stones below a certain price.

Advertise in the classifieds. Classifieds in newspapers, magazines and store bulletin boards all are effective. Newspaper classifieds are best because you can run the ad daily. Magazines are usually monthly and have one- to two-month lead times. This isn't an easy approach is you're selling loose, unmounted gemstones. The average person is totally incapable of imagining what a stone will look like in a mounting— and also doesn't have the slightest idea of how to go about getting a mounting made.

Take them to a consignment shop that specializes in antiques, jewelry and collectables. The seller obviously will want a commission of between 10%-30%, although you may be able to negotiate a lower amount depending on the quality and quantity of the stones you're turning over—plus any finished jewelry that may be included. Keep in mind that consignment shops aren't thrilled about selling loose stones. It's important that you sign an agreement specifying charges and insurance. You might also want to consider allowing the seller to discount the price. Make sure, too, that you give the shop a complete list and description of each stone consigned, indicating carefully the imperfections (do this with a diagram or drawing). For a sample copy of a consignment agreement, see the index at the back of the book.

Offer your stones (preferably mounted) to a dealer at antique flea markets, or sell them there yourself.

Find a dealer or collector with a specific interest in what you

have to offer. You'll get cash up front, but you may have to give up 50% to 75% of the current value as a commission to the dealer. For a directory of specialists and tips on selling by mail, send for: The Where-To-Sell It Directory (1993) edition), which lists dealers and collectors who will buy almost anything by mail. To order a copy, send $6.95 (postpaid) to:

Pilot Books
103 Cooper St.
Babylon NY 11702.

Have especially valuable pieces auctioned. You'll have to pay a commission and other costs, but these are negotiable and are often as low las 10% of the item's sales price. Auctions and auctioneers are in the Yellow Pages.

Some Information
on Pricing Lapidary Work

Charging the proper amount for their work is a constant, nagging problem for most gemcutters.

Here's a system worked out by the Moriarty Gem Company of Crown Point, IN. Proprietor Steve Moriarty has used a number of American Society of Gemcutters (ASG) certified cutters to do his work and he paid this (1988-89) schedule:

Base Price

Standard brilliant $20

It goes without saying that your money making success will be greatly enhanced by membership in a lapidary group. Join the American Society of Gemcutters or one of the local guilds and keep in tune with current trends.

Barion, heart, portuguese specialty cut	$30
Oval, emerald, antique pear, freeform	$25
Carat charge for above, 2 to 10 carats	$3
Bonus for exceptional quality cut	$5
Bonus for high yield without compromising cutting design. This is 40%+	$5
By this scale pricing for a 7-carat barion emerald cut of fine quality with a yield of 41% would run	$56.

Price Schedule...

Here is another price schedule (1989), offering to cut and repair stones by the Orpaz Gem Corporation in New York City gem company. This company's prices for various types of work are:

CZ—white fancy

3/cts or less	$8 per piece
3-10/cts	$3/ct
10-20/ct	$2.75/ct
20-25/ct	$2.50/ct
25/cts+	$2/ct

white round

3/cts or less	$6 per piece
3-10/cts	$2/ct
10-20/cts	$1.75/ct
20/cts+	$1.50/ct

CZ—green/blue

3/cts or less	$2 per piece
3/cts+	$3.50/ct

YAG—colored

3/cts or less	$15 per piece
3/cts+	$4.50/ct

Ruby/Sapphire

3/cts or less	$12 per piece
3/cts+	$3.50/ct

Amethyst

3/cts or less	$15 per piece
3/cts+	$7/ct

Cutting & Repairing
Precious $15 minimum
Semi-Precious $10 minimum

The above prices are published only so gemcutters may
evaluate what their American colleagues are charging for their work.
It is not intended for you to follow these prices but only to use them
as a set of comparable data.

New Design Thinking Can
Produce Cabochon Profits...

What is a cabochon? To follow the French meaning of the
word, the answer would be "egg shaped...or head shaped."

That's the form that most people envision when they hear
the word cabochon. They see a cabochon as having a polished top,
flat bottom, and oval shaped. Next, add the ready availability of
templates. Given these two aspects, it's easy to understand why
most cab cutters go for the rounded top oval shape when they get
ready to cut a cabochon. After all, cabbers were taught on the oval
shape and maybe a circle or two.

There's more, though, to cabochon cutting than forming
half-rounded egg shapes. The world of the cabochon takes in rec-
tangles, triangles, circles, crosses, hearts, trapezoids, baroque
shapes...in short just about any shape or form you can think of: even
tumbled stones sometimes qualify.

Too many stone dealers, cutting competitions, and jewelry
designers are hemmed in by their own definition. If the stone is
opaque or even translucent and doesn't have polished facets, they

In recent years, gemcutters have turned to unusual, interesting designs in cabochons. Sales results show that non-standard cab shapes attract and hold buyer interest.

reason, the conclusion is quick and predictable:

"It has to be a cabochon, therefore—" The shape must come out in traditional form.

Just tak e a look at all the commercial metal mountings available for cabochons. It's obvious that the jewelry and lapidary world is pegged to the oval shape. You'll find precious few mountings that admit to anything but the standard oval dimensions.

The American Society of Gemcutters, seeking to encourage its cabochon members away from such rigid design thinking, issued new rules starting in its 1990 U. S. Gemcutting Competitive Evaluations that encouraged creative design. Keeping its category for traditionally shaped cabochons, the Society set up special new, second judging and analysis category for custom shaped cabochons. The Society told members to cut any cabochon shape they liked as long as it didn't come from a commercial template.

The result: nine out of every 10 cabochons received for judging were still essentially traditional shapes—and the remainder were slight modifications of such shapes. In two years, the ASG received only a few truly creative or custom shaped cabochon.

So what is a cabochon? Well, it can be any polished, shaped, even un-carved broad surface gemstone whose flat-bottomed shape can probably be fitted into a prong or bezel type mounting.

Most cabochons have flat or slightly rounded bottoms. Flat bottoms—or only a slightly curved bottom—mostly in a translucent or opaque mineral, are the sina qua non of a cabochon, though.

It's also true that some cabochons have faceted surfaces (referred to usually as cabochettes). This is acceptable so long as the final stone features predominantly broad surfaces. And you can still be dealing with a cabochon when the stone is clear or transparent. Cabochon refers to the cutting style, not the stone type. Admittedly, almost all opaque stones are cut en cabochon but faceted hematite is still a cabochon or rose cut stone—when done with a flat bottom.

> **"More than shape, cabochon refers to a cutting style or technique... and this style permits much greater freedom for shaping minerals. Only in the last few years have cutters begun using this freedom."**

In the final analysis, cabochons need to be viewed as any standard or free form shape that features broad polished surfaces intended to show the texture or surface of a mineral.

For this reason, cabochon cutters should be looking at different shapes and forms from which to draw their inspiration. There are many shapes which could be developed in stone form, so creative thinking can produce an explosion of new ideas...and people.

Fabrication...

In the cabochon area, too, the fabrication or assembly or combination of stone types is a lapidary technique that is as acceptable as oiling a faceted stone to hide flaws.

Many gemcutters have reached spectacular heights of creativity with their imaginative combinations of stones. With the use of glues or epoxies, it is astonishing how many beautiful effects can be created with the mix of stones. This includes color mixes such as turquoise and rhodochrosite, or moonstone and amethyst, lapis and onyx, citrine and blue topaz, green tourmaline and agate.

For too long cabochon cutting has been relegated to the knee-jerk reliance on tradition, templates, ovals, and single mineral entities. Truth is, the long standing reliance by cabochon cutters on their trusted templates is now in serious dispute. A test on the accuracy of various plastic and metal templates showed that some 80% of the templates are inaccurate. That's right. It's virtually impossible to cut an accurate cabochon with many templates now on the market. To test any templates you now have, simply cut or measure a cabochon that you know is accurate and then try to press it through the template opening. As often as not, the result will be eye opening. You'll find that a painfully large number of the template openings are off by as much as 2mm in too many cases.

It's time to throw your template away, regardless of its cost, and make your own templates. Once you've broken the template habit, you're on the way to creative cabochon cutting.

A quick check will often reveal that those trusty plastic and metal cabochon templates aren't even accurate. Be sure to measure all the templates openings before cutting into a piece of gem material.

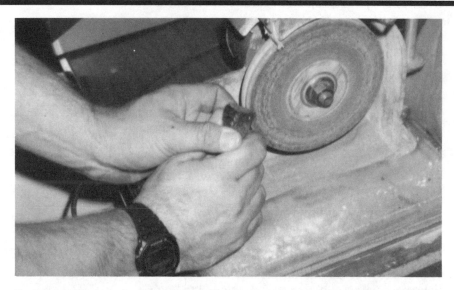

Special equipment isn't needed to fashion the new look in cabochons. A diamond dresser and a silicon carbide wheel's edge can do marvelous things.

It's time that cabochon cutting entered a new era.. The call is now out: cabochon cutters of America unite—you have nothing to lose but your shape.

A Method For Pricing Work...

By charging a flat fee plus a carat charge you are more likely to be properly reimbursed for your lapidary work, says Certified Supreme Master Duane Luce of Linville, NC.

To assure minimum income, Duane charges $35 per stone plus $1.50/ct. Thus a 5/ct stone would cost his clients $42.50.

"For a 10-carat stone and over, I charge $35 plus $1 per carat," he says. "Thus a 10-carat stone will cost my client $45 and that's any cut for any material."

On repair work, Duane usually charges $25 per hour or $25 per stone depending on the customer. Sometimes repair work is very simple (like polishing out a scratch).

Note: On repair work, make certain you get a liability release for damages IN WRITING from the client.

You Can Make Your Own Display Cases...

Every gemcutter has a selection of finished gemstones that go unmounted and, usually, undisplayed.

Placing these stones in an attractive display would enable you to show off your work.

Making a display case is not all this difficult. That you can cut a gemstone with skill demonstrates that you have sufficient hand skill to carry out a display making project.

Many different materials will suffice to make a case. One of the best—and easiest—materials would be an acrylic sheet like Plexiglass or Lexan. They are very practical for an around the home project and provide the visibility that will show off your gemstones to their best advantage.

Acrylic is lightweight, clear, tough and not too expensive. Lots of people replace broken window glass with acrylic because it won't break. Further, if your display case will be placed in your home, it's nice to know that the material represents a good safety idea, particularly

LEAVE THE PROTECTIVE PAPER ON THE PLASTIC WHILE WORKING WITH IT

AFTER SCORING THE PLASTIC, SNAP IT OVER THE EDGE OF A TABLE

USE MASKING TAPE TO HOLD CORNERS WHILE ADHESIVE SETS UP

YOU CAN BEND SMALL PROJECTS WITH A HEAT GUN

where glass and children co-exist.

Acrylic Scratches Easily...

No doubt you're already aware that while acrylic won't shatter it will scratch more easily than glass. Keep in mind, too, that it will expand and contract due to temperature changes more than glass. Allow for this expansion tendency when you cut acrylic.

If you have ever worked with acrylic you know that there are some very different procedures to follow. When you buy it, it comes with a protective paper covering on it. Always leave the plastic protected as much as possible until you are finished working with it. To cut acrylics, use a saber saw. Buy a special blade for cutting the material. If the sheet is 1/8-inch thick or less, you can score it with a utility knife and snap it over the edge of a table.To drill through acrylic, use a special bit made for acrylic. You should always clamp your work when cutting or drilling. Light sanding will give you a smoother (and safer) edge. Just be careful not to sand the surface accidentally.

To make your display case joints as strong as possible, use only the special solvent-based cement that's formulated just for the material. You will need plenty of ventilation when working with an acrylic. The cement sets up fairly fast and is thin enough to be drawn into some joints. To avoid having the cement run away from the joints and onto the surface be wary of overusing. For making corners, just position the plastic sheets however they need to be, and use masking tape to keep them in place until the cement is applied and completely sets up. Then you can remove the tape.

Bending acrylic is a little tougher. There are some special machines for accomplishing this feat. You might be able to rent one somewhere, but you can bend small projects with a heat gun. It will take some practice and the ease of heating and bending, of course, will depend on the thickness of the material you're working with.

Before you even touch the acrylic sheet, draw a full size plan for your display case on a separate sheet of paper. Transfer the drawings to the paper covering on the acrylic and then do the cutting.

Scoring will usually do a good job without fractures on straight lines. If you want a fancy, curving cut go to the saber saw.

Spucing Up Your
Repair Work...

It's no secret that clever repair jewelers will fix up a piece of gold jewelry and then give it a beautiful finish by applying as a finishing touch what is called a 24K flash.

To do a flash plating, you need to set up an electrolytic device. You can set up completely for about $10. Go buy yourself a 6-or 9-volt dry cell battery, a couple lengths of thin copper wire (say, about 12 inches long) and a glass bowl, and a 2" x .5" strip of stainless steel.

Also, buy yourself a small amount of Electro-Cleaner from any lapidary supply store. That will set you up with a electrolysis unit which just about every goldsmith shop has.

If you want to clean up gold or silver jewelry, just hook the jewelry piece up to the positive anode of the battery and the stainless

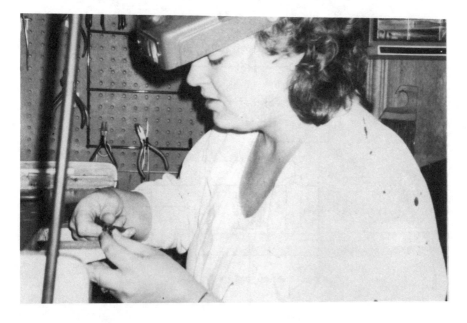

Capability at the repair bench will pay off handsomely in additional profits. Many hobbyist bench people make a fine income just working on mountings and metal smithing.

steel strip to the negative cathode. Place the two items in the electro-cleaner bath and watch the bubbles fly. It'll take about 10 seconds to give the jewelry item a fine bath.

Here's a cute trick that many goldsmiths use and it fascinates customers. Give the jewelry mounting a flash 24K plate after you've electro cleaned it. For this you'll need another stainless steel strip and another bowl (to hold the gold plating solution You can buy non-cyanide solutions from Alpha Supply, Dept. AG, 1225 Hollis st., Bremerton, WA 98310).

Note: In a home workshop you're much safer using non-cyanide type plating solutions. A touch of acid in a cyanide solution will release deadly cyanide gas.

As I said before, plating is opposite to cleaning. Just connect the mounting now to the negative cathode and the stainless steel strip to the positive anode. Now the electrical current will carry the gold particles in the solution to the negative cathode *e.g.*, the jewelry metal, and deposit it there. Presto! You now have a piece of jew-

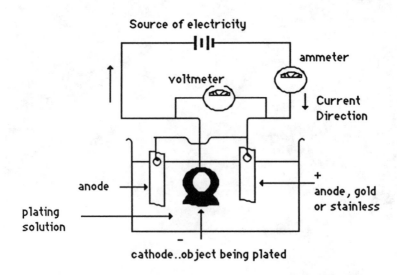

With a common 6-volt battery and a few wires, plus some gold plating solution, you can use the above diagram to set up an inexpensive plating outfit.

elry that looks like it just came off a set of polishing wheels.

Setting Up Fund Raising
With Gemstones...

Would you like to make a modest profit on your gemcutting, help the local service and professional clubs to raise money, and expand your reputation for cutting gems?

It can be done rather easily—and cheaply, too.

The idea is this: make your gemstones available on memo—at wholesale or cutters cost—to the local professional clubs and organizations in your community. Just tell the fund raising chairman that you will make your gemstones available to the club to auction off on a 50-50 basis. If you're a good cutter, such as a Certified Supreme Master or Certified Master, the clubs will jump at the chance to pro-

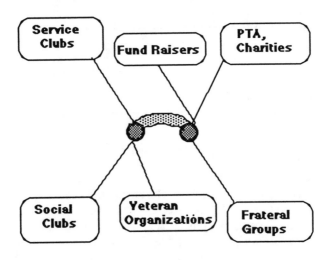

The person to contact to set up a gemstone fund raising business for charitable groups is the fund raising chairman or the club's president. A quick telephone call will usually be adequate to get things moving.

Gemstones selling at an auction represents a good profit maker for the gem-cutter, and a valuable, popular rund raising event for an organization.

vide their membership with a unique auction...and make good income for the club as well.

Fund Raisers Every Years...

Most clubs conduct an annual sale or auction each year. Church groups and local PTA's, too, are always on the lookout for ways to provide income to carry out their charitable activities. When you tell the chairman that you'd like to help out with a 50-50 auction that involves well cut, fine natural (and even synthetics although they really don't sell all that well at an auction: the real ones are what excite people!) most organizations will jump at the chance. **Note:** "Pink Ice" *i.e.*, pink CZ, makes synthetics a good auction item also.

The way to get such a program going is to make a quick telephone call to the individual responsible for fund raising such as the fund raising chairman of the organization's president. Prepare a pleasant prospect letter or a follow up letter and have it run off by the local printer or a Xerox copy machine. Explain who you are and what you propose to do for the organization. Give the club representative a reason for getting in touch with you for the good of his or her club or organization. Then end the letter with a contact notice.

Here is a sample letter:

"Dear (Mr. or Ms.):

Raising funds for the Anytown Kiwanis can be an exciting challenge—especially if you come up with a popular idea that produces good income , too.

I would like to suggest such a program.

My name is Edward Miller, of 123 Main st., Anytown. I have learned that you are the chairman for fund raising for the local Kiwanis Club here in Anytown. My purpose therefore in writing to you today is to inform you of a way to raise income for the Kiwanis at no monetary risk to you or your organization.

The program is a rare gemstone auction. It has been done in other parts of the country with great success for everyone involved. What I would like to talk with you about is offering a wide selection of superbly cut, natural, rare gemstones that your club could auction off on a 50-50 basis. I, of course, would make this selection of gemstones available to the Kiwanis on a memo or consignment basis. You simply auction off the stones, and then remit to me 50% of the price at which each stone is sold...and return to me the stones that are not sold.

Make no mistake about it. Rare, natural, well-cut gemstones are extremely popular, especially when they can be purchased at a reasonable, auction price.

I am a nationally Certified Supreme Master Gemcutter with certified membership in the American Society of Gemcutters. I can assure you that the gems are fine stones and well cut.

Would you like to investigate the possibility of conducting a "Rare Gemstone Auction" for the Anytown Kiwanis? I'd be glad to discuss the possibilities with you. My telephone number is 111-222-3333.

Thank you for taking the time to read this letter. I await your response.

Sincerely,

Charles Jones CSM"

Junk mail may irritate many Americans but it's still one of the best, least costliest ways of reaching people with your sales message.

After you've composed the letter, sit down and make up a list of all the clubs, organizations, schools, churches, etc. in your area. Try to find out if any of these entities use public projects to raise badly needed funds. If possible, get the names of the fund raising principals. Go to the local public library and look up names in the business directory.

Read the classified ads in the local newspapers. Look for the section where churches, PTA's and clubs would advertise any sales, bake offs, and other fund raising activities.

Look also in the garage and yard sales announcements. Many churches and schools and other organizations poll their membership for things that are to be donated or sold cheaply. The organizers of these activities are usually delighted to consider the possibility of conducting a rare, natural gemstone auction...particularly when it involves a local gemcutter.

Here's an important marketing tip for you, too. Don't make all your stones strictly cabochons or faceted. Get a selection of gems for the donation. The best auction is one that provides versatility.

Finally, YOU establish the minimum price at which a stone

may be sold by the organization. Don't let the organization do this unless you're merely interested in getting rid of an inventory of cut stones regardless of price. Price out your stones so they cover rough costs, your overhead and a bit of profit to you. If the stores are auctioned off at a price higher than your minimum, you and the organization will realize additional income.

Also, check the index for a sample copy of a consignment or memo agreement. You'll want to protect your valuable stones with some sort of written, contractual understanding that will stand up in court if things go awry...or threaten to go awry.

If at all possible, attend the auction with a pen and pad and the same stone and price list that was sent to the auction chairman. Keep a record of stones sold so that you can compare the club's income figures with your own. They should match up at the end of the sale. Memories get faulty and club volunteers aren't always the best accountants. The last thing you want is a dispute over money.

Not only will your attendance at the auction enable you to keep tabs on selling prices but you'll be there in case a question comes up about the stone. Bidders will often want to know just what they're bidding on and your gem expertise will be greatly appreciated by the club and the people attending the auction. It can truly be a fun way to make profits from your lapidary skills and your knowledge of gem lore.

Part III

To Market Gemstones Successfully You Must Attend to a Market Plan

By Rick Ford
mAgi

(Author's Note: Rick Ford is a professional gemcutter who also operates a gem rough dealership in Beavercreek, OR. A specialist in Montana sapphire, his marketing efforts incorporate not only rough and finished stone sales to gemcutters but also gemcutting sales direct to consumers.)

Lapidary can be a very technical thing. In marketing your gem work keep this in mind—keep your technical gobblydegook in check. The word for successful gemstone marketing is: don't over-do your know-how with lay people.

That's a fundamental rule. A little bit of demonstrated knowledge is a wonder. Too much of a good thing is a vice. Basically, when servicing a lapidary or jewelry client, reverse roles and apply the Golden Rule. If they were as familiar with lapidary and natural gemstone realities as you are, they probably wouldn't ask for your services in the first place. I've always found it wise to avoid "talking down." Keep it simple and thorough—and don't get too technical with customers. They get confused. Confused people don't buy anything until they've had a chance to clear up their confusion...and that usually occurs with someone else takes the time to explain the technicalities of gems—without confusing them further. You can impress and confuse them with all your knowledge, or you can explain enough that they can make an intelligent buying decision. I leave it to your imagination who does business with your client under those unhappy circumstances.

Explain the amethyst they've requested. Unless "created," it will have color zoning and, if they want it to emit red flashes like they've seen or heard of, they'll have to be prepared to accept the

Rick Ford, PO Box 426, Beavercreek, OR 97004, a professional cutter and rough dealer to the trade, depends on marketing for his livelihood.

necessary inclusions. These are characteristic traits. If they don't appreciate your sharing this information, then let someone else wade into such a morass.

With customers, there's usually little advantage to addressing the theoretical realm you might talk about at the local gemcutters' guild meetings. A tiny bit will impress folks that you're more than merely a hobbyist. Any more than the minimum will boggle their minds. Boggled minds are confused minds—and they'll head straight for that dependable person who can unboggle their minds and sell them something. Just don't overdo it. In selling, talk isn't cheap...it can be very, very expensive.

In selling, a salesman who talks too much loses sales. Learn to listen and make it a point that the buyer does most of the talking. That way they can give you buying and closing signals.

After all, people—including you and me—don't like their choices to be too complex or too many, no matter what they say. You do them no service by opening new corridors of possibility, unless that is what they've requested ... and that would be a rare duck, indeed! Train yourself to consciously "guide" the sale and—if you want to make more sales, therefore profit—guide them into narrowing avenues which lead to a final "yes." Customers, believe it or not, like to be brought to a commitment to buy, not into ever widening arenas of decision-making.

Stay With Buyer's Interests...

If a customer comes into your store asking for a ruby ring, it's just possible s/he wants a ruby ring. The prospective customer almost never want to be taken on a technical journey through the land of emeralds and other wonderful beryl—except after they've made a decision about a ruby ring.

Does this sound too coldly analytical? I don't mean it to

be. The science of selling is better defined than that of lapidary. No matter how good you are at your craft, the limits are engineered in, so the best salesperson, or lapidary, can't exceed designed limits. "Design" a sales philosophy, before you start and guide the sale, accordingly.

Profit implies a sale, which is possibly the first and largest problem for those of us who may be fine lapidaries, but are the rawest recruits when it comes to sales.

Again, some engineering in sweeping terms, is time well spent. Here are some questions that any good lapidary must ask. What lengths will I go to make a sale? How much profit must I have? How much is enough? When does business become too much and the fun of lapidary too little? If I decide to alter my initial objectives later, have I left myself a way of doing it?

The key to successful profits in marketing gems and jewelry lies in your ability to come to grips with your own personality, your goals, and how readily you will pursue a course of action that will produce profits.

Once you've addressed a few questions such as the above, general sales basics are next. First you'll need to sell yourself and your enterprises and then you can sell product. People are far more apt to say the final "yes" to someone they know a little about and like, or, at least, don't distrust or dislike. If you've failed to take care of these essentials, don't waste your sales efforts.

Prospecting is successful selling. Some say it's 80%. Truth is, it's 95%. The good prospect is the one you can talk to and sell to. Use your everyday life to find current and future sales, but dedicate time to prospecting, usually in person. Occasionally, phone work can substitute, if timely.

Now for some specific aids to this lapidary business. Get your pricing down firm and stick to it: charge uniformly. Therefore, friends and relatives pay the same as strangers. Think of it this way: strangers are future friends. You wouldn't want to be overcharged, so don't do it. If you didn't overcharge the strangers who became

Only practice and sustained skill will produce outstanding gemstones. Selling is fine, but stick to the gemcutting fundamentals.

friends, then by the same reasoning, you're not overcharging relatives at the same prices. And remember: relatives believe they have a right to the no-charge freebie. Explain to them, too, the services in detail, re-sell yourself, your talents and services—and your time. Rough costs you money: have your relatives been hitting you up for money, too.

Forget Discounting: It Doesn't Work...

Forget discounting. It doesn't work all that well even for the big stones. In the end, you'll work harder for their business because there will be endless questions and adjustments after the sales. And an endless stream of arguments you don't need.

Establish a minimum charge and stick to it, no matter to whom you sell, no matter how small the job. You can afford to be really fussy over the tiniest details if your minimum is two hours and, despite the finicky treatment, the job only took part of that. Usually it goes the other way anyway, so when the gravy boat comes, take some. The client will be extra pleased with the results and has agreed to the minimum fee, anyway. Also, don't skimp on packaging if mailing a finished piece. Attractive packing denotes valuable contents. Be sure to insist on—and add to the bill—special handling by the shipper such as certified mail, even if that doesn't mean insurance, per se.

Successful people ask for the sale. Sound obvious? Review your sales calls and honestly inquire, "did I let the 'time to ask' slip by?" Timing is very helpful, the sign of a polished salesperson, but failure to ask is the beginner's greatest downfall. Get the commitment to buy and firmed up in some fashion punctuated by the buyer's action, usually a check in refundable deposit. People need to be guided through decisions—even other professional people—and they'll appreciate it, without fail, when it's done gracefully.

While on the subject, all people suffer from buyer's remorse, those nagging doubts after their commitment to buy. Expect and be prepared, both before and when it surfaces.

Sending Out...

Never send out finished product you don't feel good about. It may not be perfect. The first thing one has to learn when doing lapidary "for sale" is when to quit. When to say, "enough." Perhaps you had unforeseeable problems and you feel you should have spent some additional time on the polish.

These are merely signs of nagging insecurity. Don't send out poorly crafted work, of course, but never give in to insecurity and sell your own work short.

I've spoken to full-time bona fide commercial facetors in the U. S.—folks who you can send a kilo of African amethyst to and they'll agree to cut all that's worthwhile for, say $8 per finished ct., flat. The one thing they had in common is that they insist on shipping CASH.

If that kind of commercial cutting is for you, fine! It's not for me because he who cuts by the pound simply parallels the Thai sweatshops, but for a slightly larger bag of rice per day. I want clients who'll pay for what it's worth for the best cutting job I can give them. In return, I'll observe impartially their objectives or tell them I can't do it. And then I'll do my level best to produce the kind of high quality cutting they have a right to expect.

Use Guarantee...

When I cut a gem for someone and the work is finished, I'm proud to send it out with full return privileges FOR ANY REASON, just like I do with rough sales I make to gemcutters. I steer customers away from jobs that aren't worth the cost of cutting, so I circumvent the case of anyone being stuck with something ugly. If the clients want to relinquish the goods, in lieu of the bill, I'm proud to add it to inventory for the cost of cutting. I don't want anyone unhappy with a stone that I cut. It's bad advertising and I can't enjoy the pride in my work that I strive for.

Make Your Jewelry...

Should you make jewelry? Yes and No. It can be a viable aid to sales. Who can argue with this? Gold/silver-smithing holds no appeal to me. I'd rather design and arrange trades with someone who is interested in metal work.

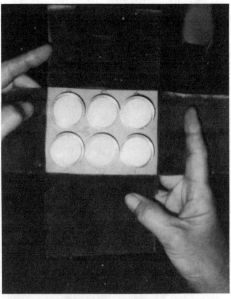

Invariably, those who try to serve two masters end up master of one, the other, or neither. I see it all the time. I'll just make this observation and move on. Not to criticize those who try, but they always choose, in the end, or just quit and simply become merchants.

Alternatives exist for people like me besides trading. I can show you a pocket-sized, display case made by the hands of gemcutter Jerk Steiner of Montana. He is among the last practicing saddlemakers, now a teacher of faceting.

In his cases, I carry jewels to the bank, coffee shops, super markets, etc. along with business cards. When someone asks me, "what do you do?" I flip out a six pack or two of faceted, cabbed,

carved gems of combined styles—blue, green, red, plus an opal—
usually stones more for an exhibition of my skills than for sale. People are ALWAYS impressed—and does it ever lead to sales.

Ask For Referrals...

Incidentally, any lapidary trying to make profits should
always ask his past and current clients for referrals. This is the first
rule in prospecting. These are pre-sold prospects and you should get
into this mode just before holidays. In my cutting, too, I try to keep
stock for up coming month's orders. A ready supply is just good
business. When August isn't far off I know that peridot will make its
annual payoff. Peridot is not all that popular with foreign cutters so
could be a perfect niche for an American gemcutter.

Here's as a final point that needs to be heard: I always crave
to learn about the details of those who claim to make grand sales of
"created" gemstone design.

In my experience, these sales are never grand, barely covering
wages, which makes it hard to justify stocking them as inventory.

Grand, magnificently cut stones are a true sight to behold.

**Yes, you may even be a certified cutter
capable of extraordinary work, but a professional
gemcutter must know how much effort can be applied
to a profitable stone...and that means knowing when to
"stop."**

One should be able to sell the merits of such gemcutting. I've
found, though, that many end users and this includes a few jewelers
don't really place that much emphasis on it. The famed GIA recog-
nizes a maximum difference between a poorly cut stone and the best
as being a mere 20% of the stone's dollar evaluation. Imagine how
little they'd value an award winning diopside.

While it's useful and important then to obtain certification as
a cutter—that CMG or CSM looks mighty impressive on the workshop wall or on a business card—don't be misled. Certification at-
tests to your skill. The market calls for what you're very apt to con-

sider "not your best work." No cutter wishes to represent himself as a Certified Supreme Master and then offer for sale stones that at best qualify as shoddy work. Still, there is a limit to how much time you may profitably devote to your cutting reputation. It's a tough call anytime. But it must be made. Know when to quit and spend your valuable time cutting the next stone. Better, spend that saved time selling.

Remember: American gemcutters aren't filling a market so much as they're creating one. That takes work, skill, and dedication.

And the old sales bromide, "...nothing happens til you sell something..." is still alive and kicking.

Setting Prices For Gemwork...

How much do you charge for your work?

Every gemcutter has his or her own schedule. Here is some more pricing information that was developed from polling a number of gemcutters at a recent rock and gem show. The dollar amounts given here represent an average of the prices that cutters charge:

FACETING

Base Price

Round Brilliant	$25
Fancy	$30
Barion, Heart	$38

Specialties

plus
Carat Charge

1 to 12 carats	$3/ct
12+ ct	$4/ct

plus

Deadline Work	$5
Preforming Your Rough	$5

CABOCHON
Standard
Shapes (Ovals, Pears, Navettes, Circles)

5x7mm — 12x10mm	$5
14x10mm — 25mm maximum	$10

Specialties
Shapes—Heart, Cross, Star, Eye, or Custom

5x7mm — 12x10mm	$10
14x10mm - 25mm maximum	$20

plus

Mohs Charge7-1/2+	$5
Phenomenon Charge	$10

   (Chatoyancy, Aventurescence, Asterism, etc.)

plus

Deadline Work	$5
Preforming	$5

   (requires sawing and shaping)

Get Deposit On Work Orders...

When someone brings you a considerable amount of work to be done, it's best you ask for a deposit before accepting the work.

There are a number of situations where the gemcutter comes off second best in a two-person transaction. Failure to insist upon a deposit ranks at the top...especially when conducting business in home workshops. They wouldn't think of pulling off a "pay you later" stunt in a store, but with a home workshop some men or women will stand there while you do the work then announce, "I'll take care of you later." Later often never arrives and if too much time passes they get indignant if you insist on being paid. The rule is: collect up front...that's RIGHT NOW! on small jobs less than $25..

One of the ways you can get hurt is when a customer or a friend brings in some rough from who-knows-where and wants you to cut some or all of it into stones. Upon completing the work, the

Rule ONE in repair take-in: never write "diamond" on a receipt or work slip just because the owner says its a diamond or it looks like a diamond. Instead, write down "white, transparent stone"—and if the owner demands a better definition, agree only to add—" which owner claims is diamond."

owner looks at the stones and announces, "So this is what they look like cut. I don't like them and I don't want any."

A good way around this would be to require a deposit before commencing with any speculative work.

Repair work—a tiny job—is where you get hurt the most. Many times a customer will come to you with a small stone out of a piece of jewelry. "Would you have a little replacement stone that you could put in?" Perhaps the task either calls for a fractional stone that you already have or you must cut one. If you can do gold-silver smithing, you might even find yourself mounting the new stone. A bit of stone setting skills, incidentally, is a handy talent and will usually pay off on small repair jobs. You should consider buying an inexpensive pair of stone setting pliers and learn to use the tool.

More than one gemcutter has learned to his or her chagrin that it would have been far easier to quote a price for the job up front. You're walking on dangerous money collection problems when you make some vague comment such as "well, let's first just see what we have." When you finish a task after such a comment you're almost always going to get stiffed with a "pay you later" promise. Let the customer know what it will cost before you start and get a commitment on payment. Be careful how you handle this because what you really should tell the customer is that you expect to be paid NOW. A good way to handle this would be, "Well, this isn't much, probably $15. Do you have that much cash on you or will you pay be check?" Yes, that sounds a bit forceful, but sometimes you want the kind of clear understanding that makes for good friends.

Cut Unique, Custom Cabochons If You Want to Sell at a Profit

By Walt Bellamy

(Author's Note: Walt Bellamy is an outstanding master gemcutter from New York and has been profitably cutting individualized cabochons for more than 20 years.)

Today's buyers of gemstones insist on originality
        I came back from a very successful rock and gem show in upper New York State this week. I sold stones—both faceted and cabochons—and jewelry like never before.
        When the three-day show was over and I counted up nearly $7,000 income (about twice what I've ever made before). It was at this show how I realized that American Society of Gemcutter Executive Director Gerald "Jerry." Wykoff was right.
        What was Jerry's advice to me about a year ago?
        "Don't try to compete with the cookie cutters, Walt," he said, "because 75 cents-a-day labor will tear you up.
        "The way for an American gemcutter to cut profitably is to go for the custom cut...the perfectly executed cut...the one-of-a-kind shape...the careful, skillful orientation of a top quality stone for its color, clarity, texture—or whatever it is that makes one stone stand out above all others.
        "Go to any contemporary rock and gem show. They're all the

same for the most part. After you've checked out one exhibit you can go home. Why? They're all selling cookie cutter goods—round brilliant or oval faceted stones mostly of poor quality, oval cabochons, emerald shapes and beads and spheres. That's it.

"If you want to make money you must cut your own path, make your time and talent pay off. Any reasonably proficient gemcutter can cut and sell a stone: it really doesn't take all that much talent. Where the American gemcutters must depart from the cookie cutters is in brainpower. They need to think out a crystal or mineral slab. By that I mean to maneuver it strategically, cut it carefully with outstanding skills and then showcase it," he said. "Once upon a time it was Americans who put all the skill and quality into gemcutting. Imported stones were notable only for their poor angles, calibration, and polish. That difference is gone now: the world cutting community is on a level playing field.

"To stand out now, you need to do standout work. For

For interesting, creative shapes in cabochons try reading the design and style magazines. Cut out designs with a razor blade and shellac them—top and bottom—to the slab surface...and start cutting.

example, jump on the current 'Buy America' craze by obtaining some high quality Montana sapphire and cutting it. An American stone cut by a talented American gemcutter...what could be a better combination?"

Take His Word...

I took Jerry at his word. Back home in my basement workshop I looked over my cut stones. Sure enough, most of the cabs had been done the way I was taught. They'd been cut from a standard template. The faceted stones were mostly traditional... round brilliants, emerald or step cuts. The cabs had the same lack of originality. They were all well cut, but—

I had to admit it. Jerry was on the money when he said buyers are "looking for something different." Look in the finished drawer of any gemcutter and most of the stones will not return a decent profit. You can't compete successfully—even if you're retired and

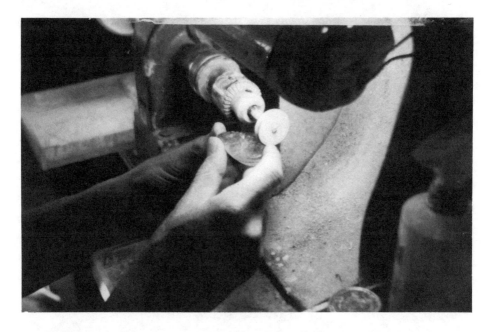

If you don't have the cutting tool that will create the stone design or cut that you want, then make a wheel out of buttons, washers, disks, etc.

don't need the money all that much— against amethyst and blue topaz cut in standard modes from the Far East. This merchandise sells from $2-$6/carat. How can anyone, even a hobbyist, compete with that—or even want to.

"Well," my wife, Anne, challenged me, "are you going to go into a change or stick with what you've been doing?"

My answer was clear enough. "I'm going to cut as many custom, unique cabs and faceted stones as I can for the next six months. Further, I'm going to put them in custom mountings instead of the Tripp settings I've been using."

Both my wife and I worked and thought up new ways to approach gemcutting. We didn't score any breakthroughs or make any inroads into new lapidary areas like the the more famous American gemcutters such as Idaho's Larry Grays and New Hampshire's Michael Dybers. We did, though, develop marvelous new shapes and treatments.

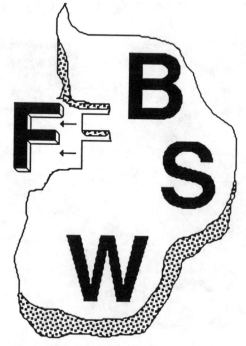

Paste-on letters or letter stencils that can be purchased in any office supply store make excellent initial templates for personalized cabs.

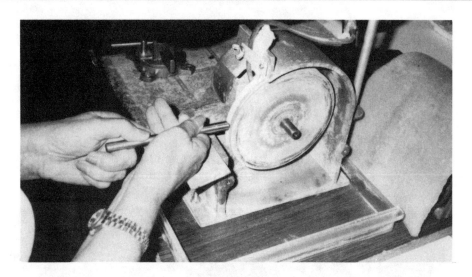

Keep your silicon carbide wheels smooth and even with a diamond dresser, but don't overdo the dressing...you waste wheels that way.

Rather than sand and polish every visible surface we experimented with frosting, two-tone effects. I carved designs into the face of the cab. I even made them with high polished surfaces and then cut—and left unpolished-various initials. (These initialed stones REALLY sold well at the shows!) We read all the old magazines that are published in the lapidary, sculpturing and art design fields. You can get some really original ideas from these magazines. It doesn't take too much in the way of altering or changing existing designs to make them workable for cabochons or faceted cuts. And you have the bonus reward of offering cut gemstones that are contemporary, that reflect current design concepts.

Copying Isn't Necessary...

I'm not talking about copying someone else's designs. I didn't need to do that. A good artist's magazine has an abundance of ideas in it. The jewelry trade journals show off the best designer's works. For me, these magazines and their four-color pictures represented simply an inventory of good, usable design ideas that I could incorporate in my own work.

It didn't take me all that long to come up with a nice line of one-of-a-kind jewelry items. I even took a try or two at sculpting, creating a few nice table top mineral items. And don't try to tell me that cabochons are hard to sell. If you cut a good one with some imagination, it'll sell.

Once I had the line, well even before I filled up an entire exhibit with my new custom items, I knew that it was working. My standard cabs and round brilliants just sat in their cases while the custom work got picked up, rolled around and looked at—and then sold. When you inlay gold or crush up some turquoise, mix it with epoxy, and then pour this into a cut cavity on a nice cabochon, well,

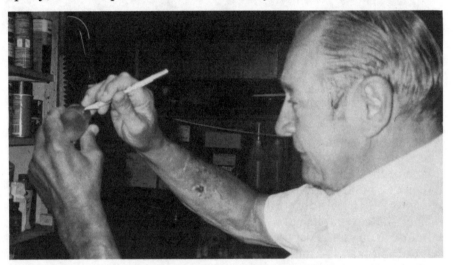

One good technique for developing unique cabochon shapes is to draw the new design on gum backed paper, cut it out with scissors and then attach and cut the design into the stone (coating with shellac).

you're getting somewhere in gemcutting then.

Funny thing, too. In shows such as I work, many potential customers want to bargain. Often, they'll try to get the price down and you just have to haggle if you expect to sell. I find now that with custom work it's much more difficult for people to hassle me on price because custom work is just too hard to price.

A customer will come to your booth and look over your

round brilliant or oval amethysts. They'll look at your $10/carat and then mention, sometimes heatedly, "the next exhibitor has stones just as good as yours and he's selling them for $2/carat." It's pretty hard to hold your price when the other fellow's cheaper stones are— at least to the naked eye—every bit as good as yours."

What makes it doubly difficult is the fact that much of the cookie cutter cutting coming out of the Orient represents first class cutting. These cutters are doing fine commercial work and they're actually selling pretty good stones for the money. It's all in the lower labor charge. Now that they have good equipment and technique, it's a pretty big order to challenge them in price.

At the gem shows, the word gets around the floor pretty quickly that one of the exhibitors is showing original work. People don't have money to throw away but they'll pay for good design. More and more gemcutters are finding out about this. So are the jewelers: they've discovered that original work will pay off much better.

As a matter of fact, I've been able to sell some of my original cabochons to jewelers. The jewelers usually have their own goldsmiths and they handle their own mounting. It's a growing market...but, remember, you still have to go out and find the buyer.

That's the first rule in business success. You can cut a beautiful stone, but nothing happens until you sell it.

By cutting original stones you can get them sold a lot easier, faster, and at a better price...one that will reimburse you for the time and talent you've invested in the stone.

A Superior Way to Make Interesting Cabochons . . .

Paul Melford, a Certified Master Gemcutter, is forever searching out new ways to create interesting—and marketable— cabochons.

He has now taken to the arts and graphics store to purchase large press-on letter templates. From these, Paul presses a letter on a slab of mineral and then carefully cuts out the letters with a slab saw and a hand diamond wire saw. He uses a diamond drill to make cutouts for such letters as "R," "O," "P," "A," "D," etc. He then finishes each letter in traditional cab style.

The backs of the letters are carefully flat lapped to assure that each letter is the same thickness. Once the letters are finished, Paul flat laps a thin mineral background piece and glues the letters onto this. Depending on how the customer intends to use and display the work, Paul glues a hook to the rear, sets up an easel prop or even attaches the stone piece to a frame covered with green felt.

In some cases, the back pieces have been made with glass. When a colored background is desired, a sheet of colored acetate is attached to the bottom of the backpiece and the stones are glued on. Paul uses a clear 5-Minute Epoxy, moving each letter in a circular manner over the epoxy until all of the bubbles have been removed. The results can be spectacular.

Which Shape Sells Best...

If you're looking at a piece of mineral or crystal and wondering what shape you should cut for the market, here

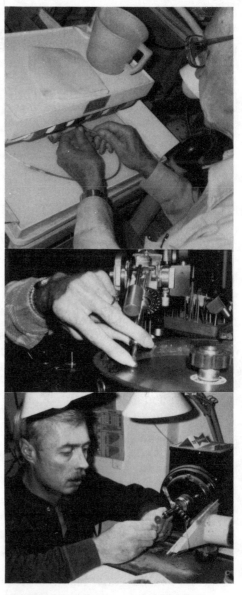

Whether cabbing, faceting, or carving stones, shape and finish always create maximum buyer interest.

are the results of a survey taken by John Christianson, of Green Bay, WI, who is a member of the American Society of Gemcutters.

A public balloting was held to determine what shapes of faceted gems were most preferred. This was conducted at the biannual rock and gem show of the Neville Public Museum geology club of Green Bay, WI, in 1993.

The display gems were all cut from clear 24% lead glass to the same approximately size and were in a Riker mount. The people in attendance were encouraged to vote by the promise than an amethyst in the shape of their choice would be cut for them if their names were drawn. The popularity results were as follows:

1.	Emerald	01.6%
2.	Navette	15.2%
3.	Pendaloque	15.1%
4.	Pentagon	10.8%
5.	Oval	00.0%
6	Octagon	07.5%
7.	Hexagon	07.2%
8.	Round	16.6%
9.	Triangle	06.5%
10.	Square	01.5%

Gem Buyers Look For Uniqueness...

Gemcutters enjoy a growing U. S. colored stone market almost every year—and it will get better through the 1990's.

Rubies and sapphires have jumped in price about 200% in less than a decade. Tanzanite, in short supply only a short time ago, is plentiful again and the price hikes aren't expected to impair the stone's popularity or signal a long term decline.

Buyers have turned the fantasy cut into more of a trend than a fad but buyers continue looking for more imaginative work, too.

As one designer emphasized, "This is the age of the Yuppie and these buyers want individual, one-of-a-kind, customized work. They're willing to pay for it...and many are becoming sophisticated gem buyers as well."

That reflects well on the efforts of U. S. gem cutters who emphasize quality cutting. The problem with most U. S. cut gems, an industry source said, is that few offer fantasy or original cutting.

As evidence, he cited the spectacular rise in sales for triangular shaped gems. These days, the trademarked Trilliant (now in public domain) and Princess—or anything close to them—sell fast and at good prices. Once strictly a diamond cut, Trilliants are now being offered in sapphire, ruby, spinel, tsavorite, and chrome tourmaline. Cutting instructions for a Princess-like stone have been published by the American Society of Gemcutters and elsewhere so this popular cut will be available to enterprising gemcutters to sell without danger of patent infringement.

The round brilliant is still the most popular cut of all, but faceters should test their own markets for triangular, Barion, Princess-like stones weighing 15 carats and above...that's where the current market for loose stones seems to be headed.

Also, keep in mind that stones of 15 carats and above outsell all other sizes. The stones that are in most demand these days include: fancy colored corundum (yellow, pink, padparadscha), spinel, pink and green tourmaline, Mexican fire opals, chrome tourmaline, blue topaz and tsavorite.

Prices to Remain High...

"The prices on mainstream stones will probably remain quite high for the foreseeable future thanks to continuing demand and relatively limited supply," says Robert Flegger of Wholesale Gems, "consequently many buyers are turning to exotic stones."

Translated into hard sales, this means that ruby and emerald sales will still turn a good profit, ditto with sapphires and aquamarines...while sales of Tanzanites, tourmaline, diopside, Sunstone, etc. are coming up fast—especially when they're well cut.

Cabs Are Making Strong Comeback...

Cabochons are making a strong comeback worldwide.

Ever since European designers began using top quality, custom shaped cabochons in their top end jewelry lines, the cab market has been alive.

Once upon a not so distant past, cabochons were utilized primarily in middle- and low-end jewelry. The reason: the stones were all cut in oval shapes of relatively poor quality materials with not too much cutter originality in bringing out the best qualities.

That's all been changed. Cabs are now being cut in rounds, ovals, hearts, triangles, pears, baroque—and the cutters are using top materials.

The bullet shape a is also gaining in popularity. Designers are going for the high domed top which is so

Rockville, MD, carver, Helen Serras, is a remarkably creative artist and her clientele includes upper crust and royaly, because her inspired work nearly sells itself.

useful for creating different effects. Thanks to the impact created by the new Munsteiner and Fantasy cuts, geometrical shaped cabochons are catching on, particularly in the ear ring market.

The future? Forecasters see a showering cascade of cabs...and the latest design wrinkle is for the fabricated stone *i.e.*, mixing of various mineral types to create a unified appearance. What appears truly interesting is the appearance of some fine synthetic gems such as lapis lazuli, opal, and turquoise.

Turquoise, incidentally, has been showing up in a reconstituted form where all the imperfections have been removed, giving the finished product the appearance of fine, Persian turquoise.

Successful Marketing of Gemstones Requires Uses of Various Techniques

Are there a variety of ways for a gemcutter to sell loose gems profitably and easily?

The only possible answer is "yes, but — "

The "but" involves effort and planning. Given these two important elements, any gemcutter can work out an effective marketing

Consider a number of marketing techniques: flea markets, personal trade sales, direct to consumers, gift-specialty shops, memo selling, etc.

Professionally designed four-color business literature is inexpensively available for use on a typewriter or computer printer.

plan that will produce enough income to continue.

Before proceeding with any kind of selling program, though, you must first resolve a few important things.

When it comes to developing a marketing plan, the gemcutter must first decide what s/he seeks to accomplish and what kind of market environment is to be created.

If, of course, you intend to conduct your marketing on a personal salesmanship basis, then a list of prospects within walking or driving distance would be a critical ingredient.

If you intend to operate on a direct mail basis you'd need not only a good list of proven prospects who buy mail order but you'd also need some good direct mail promotional literature. Do you need an expensive copy writer? Not really. Just describe your gems, price them competitively and your own literature will serve you just as well—often better—than some of the professionally prepared materials.

If you intend to use an indirect sales solicitation program such as handouts, drop cards, welcome wagon intros, stuffers, etc. the challenge becomes even less. You'll need promotional literature again, of course, but the market target becomes less of a problem. These promotional items can also be used spur of the moment. When you detect customers—or a group—you start getting your handouts to them.

If you intend to solicit jewelry stores and/or jewelry repair shops or wholesale-manufacturers, you'll need a list of stones that are available for sale and a telephone or the mailbox.

The one element that runs like a theme through all of these ideas consists of a piece of promotional literature. This can be as simple as an attractive 3x5 card or as extensive as a 4-color multi-page brochure.

> **"Attractive, professional sales and business literature denote a serious businessman, so make certain your promotional materials are the best you can make them."**

The classified ad gambit is one of the better ploys for marketing gems. With this method, you simply obtain the best repetitive ad insertion rate you can get and offer one or two stones for sale. Be brief and include a telephone number (not your name).

Prospects who scan the merchandise columns for bargains, or those who are interested in buying a gem, simply see your ad and call up. Be prepared to bargain, though, because it's often customary.

The 7 Points of Payoff Profits . . .

It takes discipline and a procedure to produce profits in lapidary. Here is the 7-step procedure formula by Certified Supreme Master Gemcutter Herb Hirata of TX, for making his gemcutting skills pay off:

- ✔ Prevent early burn out of expensive laps—by careful attention and maintenance *e.g.*, don't remove material with fine laps.
- ✔ Proper lighting—Use good, well directed lighting so

you can evaluate your work properly
- ✔ Simple dopping—Use the KISS method (Keep It Strictly Simple)
- ✔ Polish—Increase lap speed slightly when using diamond polish.
- ✔ Experience—The more stones you cut, the better mastery of different patterns and techniques you will have. It's the only "Banker's Rule" *i.e.*, you can't make any withdrawals if you haven't already made deposits. Experience and experimenting are great deposits.
- ✔ Sources for Rough and Equipment—keep everlastingly at it keep looking for new, better suppliers.
- ✔ Wholesale Buying—get yourself a state tax number (it's cheap and easy) so you can get into the wholesale buyer sections at shows and exhibits.

The Way Professionals Buy Rough is Critical...

Make no mistake about it. If you buy your rough well the profits are built in. Buy poorly, and—

It makes a difference when you buy rough at a low price per carat or gram and then are able to obtain a high price when cut. Surprisingly enough, effective yield will often return a better profit than will pricing per carat.

Good rough has a price known to miners, dealers, and cutters. They know what a specific piece of rough should cost. Further, they have a good idea what kind of price the mineral will bring when it's cut properly. You won't fool too many dealers.

The profit making gemcutter knows how to buy rough. That holds true whether the buy is being made upon personal inspection of the rough or mail order.

The best advice that can be given to a gemcutter about to purchase rough is: "be realistic about what's available." All the talk you've been hearing lately about no good rough left is just talk. What's available at any given time, though, or from any particular dealer is another side of the issue.

Remain Flexible in Rough Purchases...

Every dealer doesn't have exactly what you want at the time you want it and in the amounts and price you want. So be flexible in addition to realism when dealing with a rough dealer.

A cutter should focus on a nice piece of tanzanite rather than a 5-carat stone from which he hopes and expects to extract a 4-carat cut. You aren't going to get rough in near pre-form shape every time. Often you'll pay for shards and points that must be removed. That's why the effective yield over time is only about 25%. When a gem-cutter brags an average yield of 50% he can expect to impress only the amateurs. Professionals who deal with rough know better.

Any successful ongoing gemcutting business is situated on the foundation of effective rough purchases and then maximum yield from cutting.

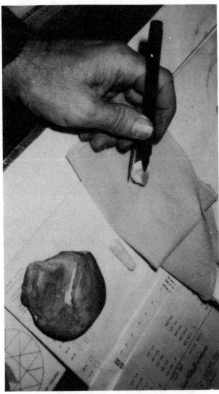

Invest some time managing rough. Check measurements and optics carefully so your cutting will truly reflect the jewelry truism, "The metal work will sell the piece but the gemstone will produce the profit." Get the best yield, of course, but first get the best possible gemstone that the rough will allow. Let the rough's original shape make most of your cutting decisions: so you'll make profits. With high value rough, experienced gemcutters allow the rough to determine the cutting shape or design. Remember: not all rough comes in nice, manageable chunky near-preforms.

Expecting an 80% yield out of a piece of rough represents poor thinking. It's not realistic to begin with and the rough supplier shouldn't be held accountable for an expectation like that.

Set realistic specs for your rough purchases and then allow the rough dealer to work for you—not against your specs. If a gemcutter locks a dealer in on every specification of a stone, including size, then the dealer will probably need to find a crystal that meets those specs by cutting or sawing larger pieces.

If, on the other hand, the gemcutter shows flexibility on some of his or her specs, then perhaps on an order for a 15-carat stone, the dealer can return one at 12 carats...but with a better color. This way, the gemcutter gets the better of the bargain. Don't forget either that some material just won't cut for size. Some garnets and diopside must be cut small so why order large chunks. You're defeating your own purpose when you do that.

Most professional rough dealers can hit the mark on any given set of specifications. They know stones. It's their bread and butter. There may be some compromises in order to meet a series of strict specs, but if the gemcutter will respond to the dealer's professionalism, h/she will usually end up with a much better stone purchase. So far as being offered some sad fragments keep in mind that by toning down the expectations you stand a much better chance of being happy with your rough purchases. Gem rough just doesn't always come in the precise shape and size that you order. Once you understand that you'll have less difficulty with a dealer.

A piece of rough isn't all that attractive anyway, not even to an experienced cutter. Even some of the finest pieces don't appear sensational in the rough state. It's only later when they become swans that a cutter or prospective buyer can see the real beauty.

Unreasonable Expectations...

One dealer emphasized that his biggest problem with gemcutters—even experienced professionals—is the buyer who insists, "I want a piece of X size." A dealer can have a larger piece and then he must saw it to conform to the order. That's something no dealer likes to do. It's tough to hit the exact carat weight on the nose. So the billing is bound to be slightly over and/or under on most occasions. A gem rough buyer should expect this. Dealers agree that the gemcutter who gives them the most trouble is the one who insists on ordering specific sizes. If you order a 5-carat piece from a dealer—no more and no less—then that 5-carat piece may have irregular features that must be cut away, perhaps leaving you with a 1-carat finished stone. The cutter who orders a a 5-carat piece and is determined that he'll cut a 3 or 4 carat stone out of it is usually playing mind games. In most instances, it just isn't going to happen.

The smart gemcutter will develop a trusting, on-going relationship with a good rough dealer and then use the latter's professionalism and experience to insure profitable purchases.

Because nature and circumstance provide rough, you should learn to trust your rough dealer. Use his years of judgement and experience—and especially his stone inventory. If a dealer ships you a stone with 3 extra carats of weight and bills you for the extra, take a hard, mature look at the rough. It might fit your needs better than a fragment that just happens to meet your order—but not your wants.

Don't forget that large orders are easier to fill than small ones. You'll generally get better merchandise on a larger order, and not just because the dealer sees greater income. If you order 100 carats or 100 grams of chrome diopside and you want clean, chunky crystals, a dealer can better fill that order to your satisfaction then he can on a single stone.

Costs on Specified Orders?

Does it cost you more when you specify an order?

It depends. If a dealer has a piece for a specified order, fine. On an 18x16mm size order, the dealer knows he almost certainly faces a money loser. He can't really fill such an order without cutting up larger materials. Because price of gem materials, whether rough or cut, rises geometrically with each arithmetic increase in

In estimating potential yield from a piece of rough, the value of the rough is an important element of the equation. Blue topaz is inexpensive so it can be shaped as needed: ruby is another matter.

size, it just doesn't pay to cut down.

If you're an old time customer, the dealer will probably do it for you—after exhausting attempts to convert you to some realm of reasonableness. He'll want you to expect something a bit less or a bit more...not precise.

You can hold a dealer's feet in the fire if you know him and have dealt with him. Don't try those tactics on a dealer you don't know. He'll probably refuse the order. No one likes to deal with disagreeable people.

The Profit Markup Formula...

Once you have your rough, what's the true markup formula. Sofus Michelsen, a Certified Master Gemcutter from New Jersey, says the 6-time markup formula of rough to finished cut will assure a profit.

Is this true?

Probably, yes. It's the minimum, though. Figure the markup this way: if a gemcutter buys a 20-carat piece of rough at $10/carat, he'll have invested $200. If the cutter realizes a 7-carat finished yield at $60/carat, he'll realize $420 on the stone. That's the jewelry industry's normal keystone markup *i.e.*, double the cost.

Is keystone worth it to you? That's a decision you'll have to make. The important element of this discussion is this: know your costs and yield. Some gemcutters will be satisfied with a keystone markup and others may want more or less.

For gemcutters willing to take a risk on a "gambler's stone" there are the emeralds and rubies. The cost per carat in the rough is so high that a gemcutter can't afford to miss on the call of color, clarity, and imperfection position. Experienced cutters appreciate the dangers lurking inside which the closest analysis and inspection often won't reveal. On a gambler's stone you can risk $100 a carat for rough and maybe realize more than $1,000 a carat without difficulty.

A $15/carat chrome tourmaline, a pariaba tourmaline or a bi-color tourmaline also represents the same throw of the dice, but on a much lower scale. If you've ever purchased an opal you know what a gambler's stone is.

Other gambler stores upon which an enterprising gemcutter might want to risk a few dollars include sapphire, tsavorite, tanzanite. With a tanzanite it's often difficult to know if there's an embedded inclusion that will pop when you heat treat the stone. Tsavorite is also great at hiding trouble making flaws. As for sapphire, you really aren't too certain what you're buying—unless you're buying the highly profitable and easily sold Montana sapphires—because you're uncertain what the color will be until it's been color oriented or cooked. Even with blue sapphire rough, the final color seldom looks like the rough's color.

Marketing Gemstones: Where Are the Buyers?

The first question asked by every gemcutter with stones to sell; is, "I know there are many people who want gemstones so why am I having so much trouble selling any of my stones to them profitably?"

It's a fair question—but a very difficult one for someone without professional sales experience. Selling gemstones is not all that difficult when you have a good marketing plan and the personal

talent to carry out your marketing plan. You need only walk around in Tucson some February to realize that a number of people are making excellent money selling gemstones. Also in Tucson you'll find an equal number of them who would consider themselves lucky if they even covered expenses.

Here are a few simply-to-carry-out marketing plans that gem cutters can try:

The Window Trick...

Regardless of your present situation, you should be aware that nothing will happen until you sell something. That means you simply must get up out of the cutter's chair and put on a salesman's hat.

One enterprising gemcutter in Chicago does it this way. He has printed up a number of attractive 3x5 cards with these words.

> **If you would like to learn something about buying —at gemcutter prices—some of the world's finest cut natural gemstones to feature in your jewelry, please call 111-111-1111 for my free recorded message. I cut and sell my own gemstones.**
>
> **Charlie Jones CSM***
> ***Certified Supreme Master Gemcutter**

In his home, the gemcutter has hooked up a small answering machine with a 30-second message. The phone-machine hookup runs 24 hours a day unattended (the gemcutter needs to change cassettes now and then).

The message on the recorded explains that he is a Master certified gemcutter * and has gemstone inventory that he would like to sell at an attractive price. If the callers are interested, they need only to leave their telephone number, or mailing address, and the gemcutter will get back to them by phone or mail with a price list on available stones as soon as possible.

And does he ever sell gemstones that way. People aren't worried about getting a sales argument with a recorded message. Once they glance at his card, it goes into their pockets or purses and a call

*The American Society of Gemcutters conducts a national certification program for gemcutters. Lapidaries who hold the coveted certification degrees (CSM=Certified Supreme Master Gemcutter; CMG=Certified Master Gemcutter, and CJM=Certified Journeyman Gemcutter) have successfully completed a comprehensive written gemological examination and submitted their work samples to a 5-person judging panel over a two-year period.

Locations for "call me" cards include supermarket bulletin boards, computer bulletin boards, club message boards, small space display advertisements, meeting places...anywhere people go and congregate.

is made...often just to find out how this interesting and amusing marketing idea is carried out.

How does he get distribution on the cards? The gemcutter devotes a couple of afternoons in the parking lots—especially the areas close to jewelers—and just slips his card under the windshield wiper of the car's front window. When the owner returns to the car, he can't miss the card and it only takes a second or two to read the entire message.

Keep the messages—card and recorded telephone—short and sweet. These two elements produce attentiveness.

The idea has proved so practical, that the gemcutter is now running his card in the Yellow Pages, the newspapers and local magazines. Even jewelers call him up now and ask for prices on specific stones.

"Blind Man's Bluff" Marketing...

The gemcutter has other techniques for getting his "call me" cards distributed. When a gem and jewelry or rockhound show is scheduled, he makes certain he's in attendance talking with people and handing out his cards. His favorite trick is to walk up to people in a cafeteria or luncheonette area, smile, say "hello" and hand them a card—just like some blind or handicapped people do when handing out cards that ask for a donation. He then walks on without another word or blue suede sales pitch.

What makes this simple, inexpensive little sales plan aproach so attractive is that it can literally work by itself. The only time the gemcutter gets involved is when a prospect calls up, listens to the pre-recorded message, and then follows up with another telephone call to you to show interest in a stone or stones.

What makes the "call me" approach so effective is that people know that they can call up and get a "free" recorded message without fear of a salesman beating on them.

Then it's up to the gemcutter to describe the merchandise and state a price—or arrange a personal meeting at some public place (this is safe for the prospect and the gemcutter with his expensive inventory). The street smart gemcutter NEVER invites an unknown person into his home workshop. When dealing with strangers, you simply have no idea of the character of some individuals and it's best to meet in well-lit public places *i.e.*, public library, stores, public building lobbies, etc.

Direct Mail Sales...

Another approach to gem sales is through the direct mail option.

Admittedly, postage charges have been going up in the last few years and this makes direct mail operations more expensive. If you work out the correct kind of program, though, the cost is not prohibitive and you could end up with a rather substantial profit.

New York gem dealers have worked out the direct mail approach rather well. They work off a 4-color brochure and what is call a "bounce back." Other gem and rough dealers—the successful ones—send a regular letter or newsletters to their clients, keeping them informed on prices, spinning off some homespun philosophy, and in general showing themselves to be hardworking, honest, interesting people. A shining example of this kind of dealer is Fred Rowe III of the House of Onyx fame. No one in the lapidary industry puts out a tabloid quite like Fred's—and the Tennessee gentleman is a multi-millionaire.

By working with name list brokers, gem dealers rent names at prices of about $50 per 1000 and higher. Before buying the names, they specify the characteristics that they want in the names. For example, if selling gems through the mail you obviously are better off renting names of people who have previously purchased through the mail. Also, you'll want the names of people who have purchased jewelry (not too difficult to obtain). Don't bother trying to get the names of people who have purchased only gems in the mail. Dealers who have these name lists don't rent them...certainly not to other gemstone dealers.

Direct mail is so popular with marketers because of the ease with which you can buy lists of names of people in your marketing area who have a history of buying gems and jewelry

---

It isn't always necessary to rent or buy names. Often you can compile your own lists from neighborhood directories, acquaintances, referral names from others, professional compilers, etc.

Once you have a list, you can make up a direct mail packet which, stripped to essentials, consists of:

1) Cover letter
2) Brochure
3) SASE

Use your cover letter to introduce yourself and your gemcutting service. The brochure will dramatize your offer, provide vital information on stones available, prices, guarantees, etc.

You don't always need to provide a Self Address Stamped Envelope (SASE), but the convenience of not having to hunt around for an envelope can increase your response rate. Tests have showed that providing pre-paid postage to the respondent generally has no impact whatsoever on the rate of return. If people want to respond they will provide their own stamp.

Test your direct mail package first. Do your best to get at least more than 250- names and addresses. That way you'll qualify for Third Class Mail (bulk or junk mail) which is much less expensive. **Note:** Think hard about the impression you want to make with any of

your prospective customers before deciding on whether to use First Class or Third Class mail. First class is much more acceptable to people who are inundated with bulk *i.e.*, "junk" mail. The latter signifies a rather impersonal "play-it-by-the-numbers" approach. If you're mailing to people you know, use First Class Mail. Recipients of First Class Mail aren't nearly so ready to be incensed with a sales presentation as they are when you offer arrives with the rest of the mail box stuffers.

New Hamshire's Michael Dyber is internationally renowned for his creative work, and he displays it with a stunning, well organized and imaginative booth at the annual Tucson Gem Show. Selling is as vital as creating, he realizes.

Weigh your mailing package. It's foolish to let the weight go over an ounce. Doing so will double your mailing costs.

A quick printer can print your literature up quickly and at moderate costs. Something you could think about seriously to save money is to have your entire package printed on legal size paper (11x14), triple folded, and then mailed out as a self-mailer. This way you'd be able to include all the information and have on only one printed item...and which is much easier to keep under one ounce in weight.

It's really surprising how much copy and how many illustrations you can get into a single legal sized sheet.

It goes without saying that your company literature should reflect a quality operation. For that reason, avoid if at all possible a straight black printing or copy machine rendition of your letterheads, cards, etc. Pieces that are done this way are cheap, they look cheap —and they are interpreted as cheap.

> **"You don't have to spend a lot of money on expensive looking sales and business literature. Give careful consideration to buying pre-printed stock and then typing or printing your own sales message."**

Here's an excellent tip...and it will work wonders whether you use a computer (which the pre-printed items are intended for!) or a typewriter. There is a company in Lindhurst, NJ, called PaperDirect who pre-prints magnificent four-color paper "empties" which you can fill in and instantly create professional-looking custom color brochures, mailers, letterheads, business cards, envelopes, etc.

You may purchase individual selections or harmoniously integrated packages of business literature. Once you have these pre-printed pieces your only requirement is to print in with black ink the sales message. The result? You will look professional in less time, for less money and with better results.

The company has an excellent four-color catalog and for an investment of only a few dollars and a few moments of your time you can possess a truly professional face to the buying world. To contact PaperDirect, call or write:

> PaperDirect
> 205 Chubb av.
> Lyndhurst, NJ 07071
> 1-800-A-PAPERS (this is an order number)

Keep in mind that the company's product is intended for computer printer (preferably a laser printer) use. If you don't have a huge mailing goal, the typewriter may do in a pinch.

Here is an illustration of the PaperDirect catalog which lists some rather impressive business correspondence "empties" to be filled in by you.

Quick Test...

Many gemcutters prefer to establish a customer list among the jewelers in their area.

Admittedly, the best way to accomplish this is by personal sales calls or by reference to the local library's commercial directories. In other words, develop a relationship with a jeweler who will insist on knowing with whom he's doing business. This is good advice. Collect your best work and arrange it tastefully for presenta-

If you have a computer—IBM or MAC—you can finish up the pre-printed "empties" fromPaperDirect to produce professional looking literature.

vice. Collect your best work and arrange it tastefully for presentation.

Your work is your best sales pitch. Open the case and show the jeweler the kind of work you are capable of performing. Have a few stones prices inexpensively...just so you can sell him "something" and thus establish him in your and his mind as a customer. This makes it easier on subsequent visits to sell the jeweler something: he or she has purchased successfully from you before so you are not a stranger and psychologically you have established a gentleman's agreement to work with each other.

Jewelers Need Reliable Resources...

One important capability you should impress on the jeweler is your ability to repair gemstones and to cut custom cuts. With you as a resource, the jeweler will now know that he or she can profit by offering to customers the privilege of individualized gemstones... particularly a custom cut birth stone. Impress on the jeweler, that you can expand his inventory—at no cost—many times because the store can now offer just about any gemstone in the world...without requiring the jeweler to stock up expensive inventory.

All the jeweler now has to tell a customer is "...well, if you don't see anything here that catches your fancy, please know that we can arrange to have any stone you wish cut quickly and inexpensively by a certified gemcutter..." The jeweler needs only to have a pricing list from you and the store markup can quickly be calculated before the order is even sent in to you. This is a capability for extra profits that is seldom lost on a profit minded jeweler—and such an arrangement works well for both of you.

Don't overlook the repair shops. They are constantly in need of stones and repairs. Most repair shops concentrate on metal: they don't know the first thing about cutting a stone. Your cutting shop can be a welcome and reliable resource...and most repair shop owners will be delighted to make your acquaintance. Call on the various jewelers and repair shops and let them know that you're interested in doing gem cutting work for them. If you've qualified for a rating by the American Society of Gemcutters, be sure to let the prospect know how peers evaluate your cutting talents.

When calling on jewelers and repair shops, don't forget to leave your business card and your pricing schedule. Many gemcutters forget to do this—and these two items represent the best liaison between the two of you.

Set your prices—then provide good service and work.

Chicago Gemcutter Specializes In Unique Cabochon Shapes, Textures

In many commercial markets, designers are looking for unique, customized cuts. This makes it rather difficult for the traditionally shaped cabochons but not necessarily so for those cutters willing to strike out in new directions.

Paul Feldner of Chicago, IL, is a professional cab cutter who fills his cases with unique shapes when he goes calling on jewelers and designers.

"There is nothing like an unpredictable display case," he says, "to kick up the interest of a jeweler, repairman, or designer. By unpredictable case I mean a case full of unique, customized shapes in stone. Row upon rows of traditional oval cabs won't usually get you a second look on a sales call.

"Fill that case with crosses, leaf shapes, stars, hexagons, trapezoids, triangles, off center circles—in short just about any shape you can manage to cut into a cab and you'll get excited interest—and buying motive."

Feldner cuts for a number of jewelry retailers in the Chicago area. Many of the cabs he's requested to cut, especially from designers, are mere shapes sketched out on a piece of paper. Even when he's not cutting on order, though, he invests his materials and time into new, unique shapes. Once he has a good supply of uniquely shaped stones, he makes up an attractive case or two and goes sales calling.

"The jeweler is your bread and butter," the Chicago gemcutter says. "They are in the market constantly or looking for something that can be put into a nice piece of jewelry and sold. For market research, there are no better individuals to call on than jewelers. They're in the jewelry selling business every day taking orders and rejection. Better than anyone else in the industry, they know what customers want and don't want. Even when I call on a jeweler and come away without selling at least something, I get good information from almost every call. They tell you what's going on—and that's something you just can't get working alone in your workshop.

Make Sales Calls
to Sell, Learn...

"My advice to any gemcutter is: get out and call on jewelers. Most of them are wonderful people and they love to share their information on the market with you. Sooner or later, those sales calls pay off. If the jeweler likes and trusts you, he'll almost always buy at least something from you...just to keep you coming back to his store. A gemcutter is a valuable resource to any jeweler."

And what about calling on repair shops and designers?

"They're dynamite prospects," Feldner says. "Every repair man either has a need right now for a stone—faceted or cabbed—or will have one in the near future. If he knows you and has a good idea

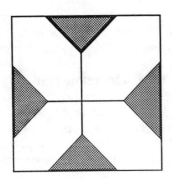

The popular square cross is easily cut out of a block of mineral using the corner of a silicon carbide wheel to remove the wedges..

of the quality of your work, you can best the house rent that he'll be calling you.

"It's surprising to me how many gemcutters don't consider the repair shops. These people are goldsmiths, not lapidaries, and they want and need to have contacts with people who can cut or fix a stone. For the most part, they keep minimum inventories of stones but they will call you and place an order.

"Repairmen are good designers, too. I make every effort to find out who's designing in the area because they're fun to work with. Just show them a unique stone and their creative mind kicks into high gear and they'll mentally design a piece while they're fingering one of my nice, custom shaped cabs. It's seldom that I don't sell one or two stones when calling on a designer.

"But keep the rule in mind: it's the unique cabochon shape or a nifty handling of texture that turns on these people. Standard oval shapes can be purchased anywhere and almost any price. Heck, when you can buy something in bulk why bother with a gemcutter."

Square Cross Popular...

One of the shapes that easily finds a buyer is the square cross. This design is little more than a standard square cabochon with four identical wedges cut out.

What makes this particular cut so popular is the powerful symbolism of the cross, dating back in history. The shape shown here is generally known as the Cross Urdee. It is also known under the names of the Passion Cross as well as the Cross of Suffering.

Note: When you're making a sales presentation on someone, don't hesitate for a second to use the name of the cut. They're exotic names and buyers respond often to what a thing is called or named just as much as they respond to the thing itself.

To get the symmetrical shape, draw out the pattern on a doubled thick piece of paper. This pattern can then be glued directly onto the top of a flat section of cabochon material, or it can be transferred via carbon paper or by scratching with a sharp tipped aluminum awl.

If you carbon the design or trace a paper cutout on the mineral, it would be a good idea to paint over the drawn lines with clear fingernail polish or shellac. This eliminates the possibility of "finger erasing" or water washing the design away.

The key to an accurate cross is the care you use in getting the shape transferred to the cabochon flat. Once you have the shape outline drawn on the stone use some shellac over it to protect it.

The quickest and easiest way to cut out the square is with a trim saw. Saw close to the drawn lines but on on them. Final sensitive shaping will be cone with a cutting wheel.

With the basic square complete, saw out the four V's, cutting close to the lines but not on them. Stop just short of the right angle. Remember that your saw blade is round and by stopping just short you avoid any interior undercutting. If your saw platform is level with the arbor you won't have an undercutting problem. Otherwise, make a slotted wedge with the wedge slot pointing directly at the blade. The slot will allow you to saw the square

cabochon deeply into the blade and remove the V's without undercutting.

Keep Wheel Edges Sharp, Dressed...

With the preliminary shaping out of the way, make certain that the edges of your cutting wheel are at right angles. Without too much difficulty you can now grind the edges down to the line (using a measuring gage to check dimensions) and then cut out the V's neatly. Cut slowly here to avoid rounding of edges.

Use a 220 wheel on the initial shaping and then finish up with a 600 wheel. Grind the dome just as you would any square cabochon. Give the work a final prepolish sanding and then polish. In the sanding operation, blunt the edges along both sides of the V's because will will soften the break between the sides and the dome.

When it comes to selecting material for a square cross the gemcutter has options to show creativity. As you do select patterns don't forget that simply rotating a square cross in wearing use will

radically change the appearance of the cab. Many materials with ver-
tical striations and banding make attractive square crosses *i.e.*, tiger-
eye, ages, rhodochrosite, rhodonite, Jade, labradorite, etc.

Consignment Selling Growing Despite Financial Dangers...

More and more gemcutters are getting clipped by dishonest
consignment retailers and dealers. Despite the dangers, though, consignment demands are increasing.

Setting up a consignment operation should occupy a top
priority for gemcutters looking to realize profits from their work. It's
all and good to demand immediate payment when completing a
gemstone transaction. For retailers, though, the cost of "floor planning" an extensive gem inventory can be excessive. Hence, many retailers seek out consignment or "memo" selling.

> **"Consignment selling can be very profita-
> ble—and also a bit dangerous because
> you're turning over your stones to some-
> one. Be sure to read the index for a sample
> consignment agreement—and get it signed
> and filed properly."**

Consignment or memo selling is a simple concept. The seller
will pay his supplier only when and if the article is sold. The dealer
accepts—without paying up front and usually for a specified period
of selling time—finished jewelry or gemstone merchandise for the
purpose of selling it. If s/he succeeds in selling within the agreed
upon selling period, then everyone gets paid. If not, the merchandise
is returned to the owner-gemcutter.

Is consignment selling for you?

That depends. Certainly, you are taking all the risk. You—
not the dealer/retailer—absorbs the financial risk of selling. You
must buy the rough, cut it, and deliver it to a consignment dealer.
You agree upon the price, the commission that the seller will re-

ceive, and the time period upon which the sale must be made.

It stands to reason that if the stone is sold you will be reimbursed. If the stone is not sold, you get your stone investment back and must decide on what or how to sell or dispose of it.

Consignment Selling Tricky...

Most jewelry industry proponents see no impending reduction in the level of consignment sales. Despite incidences of chicanery, many actually continue to look for consignment opportunities.

Why the increase? Dealers and retailers are looking for every way possible these days to reduce their cash outlays. Buying gemstone inventory even at cutter's prices is a good way to reduce your cash reserves. Jewelers understandably are not enthusiastic about that. The answer thus seems to be: let the gemcutter, wholesaler or manufacturer carry the floor planning load. ("Floor planning" refers to the interest, cash and overhead money cost of keeping inventory available for sale.) It's commission sales anyway you look at it—and sometimes the gemcutter or dealer never gets paid. That's the tough

part about this aspect of marketing.

Consignment or memo selling is said to make merchandise more expensive for retailers—and ultimately the consumer. But that's the way it is now in the jewelry industry and many practioners want to keep it that way.

How a New Orleans Cab Cutter Makes Good Living Marketing...

If you've been to the Tucson Gem Show, you may have seen him working a booth of fine cabochons. Not only will you find Tom Brissel working hard in the booth, but in the non-booth hours you're likely to see him working the crowds and lobbies, handing out flyers and direct mail pieces.

This man works hard at his gemcutting profession—and he understands full and well that nothing happens until somebody sells something. It's a poor year when Tom Brissel does less than $100,000. He goes to shows in a top-of-the-line Cadillac (he's a Buy America First fanatic!) that's never more than three years old.

"My cases are in the rear trunk—or shipped ahead," says non-camper Tom. "I wouldn't be caught dead in one of those silly camper things."

The Tucson Gem Show—a bonanza for some (like Tom Brissel), a disappointment for others, and so-so for most—represents a major income event for Brissel. He lives and works from his suburban New Orleans home, but it's the center of operations. Tom makes certain that half of the year is spent whirling about the country like a stone on the end of a string selling his line of superbly executed, customized cabochons.

With his wife, Donna, Tom keeps his diamond cab machines busy. He does the roughing, shaping and prepolishing and Donna applies the mirror-like polish finish. The polish is mostly accomplished with a sequenced set of diamond polishing pads.

With Tom Brissel, success in gemcutting came after he used his lapidary hobby to keep food on the table after being laid off from an automotive worker job. For him, selling is the major element in any successful lapidary business. You can design and cut the finest

Any profit seeking lapidary should regularly pay a visit to a rock and gem show to review the products offered and evaluate the pricing structure.

stones in the world. Until you take the time and patience to develop your own selling plan and exchange your work for hard earned money, lapidary will remain just a hobby.

Self Studies to Learn Selling...

There's nothing tricky or unique about what Tom does. He never bothered asking other lapidaries how they made a success in the business. There aren't that many making good money, he insists. To help himself out, he simply bought a couple of books on selling, laid out a plan of selling work and then worked his plan. He's been making good profits ever since.

Tom insists you won't make any money at the lapidary business unless you sell your work. And you won't sell your work unless you get people to look at it.

It's work to turn out nice cabochons, he admits. It's harder work to sell them at a price that pays you reasonably well for the time and effort you put into the cabochon cutting—and the selling.

The way Tom got started was to look up all the area repair men and designers in the Yellow Pages. He placed a personal telephone call to each and arranged to come around and visit them with cases of his cabochons. He knew once they laid eyes on the imaginative shapes and treatments—and the incredible mirror finish— some sales would result. He was right.

Note: The first thing Tom needed when he started out was attractive display cases. A quick visit to the local Sears store produced a set of rich looking, and inexpensive, brief cases. Tom glued strips of painted balsam wood for multiple shelves on the interior walls. On the shelves, Donna placed display cards which she'd made by attaching black felt to stiff particle board cut outs. The Brissels then attached the cabochons—by type and texture—to these boards using a touch of hot wax. That way, Top could slip out five or six of the display trays and the stones would remain attached in neat rows. If Tom really needed to remove a stone—and this was seldom unless it was purchased—he could pick it off easily without fear of damage to the stone or the display pad.

Not only excellent lapidary work but attractive, well thought-out displays account for success. Customers note, he says, how you handle your own stones and assign value on what they observe.

"I used some gum backed label paper," Tom explains, "and for each stone I wrote the name of the cut (and some of these were admittedly fancied up!), type of mineral, shape, weight, and the price. I keystoned all the prices from the rough price I paid originally. I always put retail keystone prices on my merchandise."

Why put retail keystone prices on the stones?

Tom explained that this was his own psychological stunt. If he's negotiating with a dealer, the dealer knows his price is half of what's on the label and it gives him a feeling of getting a better price without asking. If a retail customer happens to get near when Tom is talking with a jeweler in his store, neither Tom nor the dealer must justify wholesale prices. The retail price—or at least the keystone price—is already on the label.

Tom feels that if he had net prices on the labels it would be

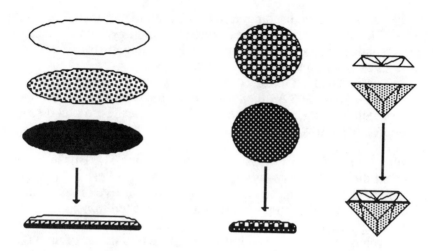

Fabricated, assembled and combination type cabs—and sometimes faceted stones—open up many new design capabilities.

somewhat difficult to convince anyone that their consumer price is, say, $10 for the cab but someone else could get it for only $5.

For the most part, Tom deals only with loose stones. He occassionally will drop a stone into a mounting. When dealing with jewelers, repairmen, and designers he concentrates on stone sales. He does this because it's easy to tie up an excessive amount of money in settings and mountings. Tom has found that to be a bit wasteful when dealing with the trade. They often prefer their own mountings—without another markup middleman involved.

Tom and Donna work the convention business, too. When a major national convention comes into New Orleans or any of the nearby cities, Tom takes a careful look. Here, he will sell finished jewelry.

"If you're going to make money at this business," he says, with some feeling, "you must make up your mind about what the market is.

"I don't think you're going to be successful selling loose or unmounted stones to anyone but a person in the jewelry trade. They know what to do with loose stones: consumers don't and they can't even imagine anything that you try to describe for them. 'Show me a picture or a sketch,' is what they say. They aren't going to buy anything until they see what it is...so why bother."

Jewelry for Consumers...

The reason for the shift in marketing is that Tom knows few loose stone sales will result when dealing directly with consumers. They don't have the ability to combine stones, mountings and the like. Further, they don't have the creative imagination to do it either. Combine these two disadvantages with the fact that they don't understand gemology all that well either, and Tom knows he'd gets lots of looking—and no buying.

Therefore, when he sets up at a local convention or meeting or even a rock and gem show for consumers, Tom displays finished jewelry. It's a special kind of finished jewelry, though. The goal is always to minimize the amount of metal needed to make a piece of jewelry. As a result, he uses a lot of rings, pins, posts, and upeyes.

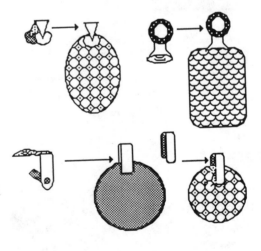

"The old saying in the jewelry business is: the stone will make your profit, the gold will sell the piece. So I try to concentrate on the stone and keep my mounting and goldsmithing to a minimum. Remember, I'm a gemcutter first, not a goldsmith. I sell

Some imaginative use of bails, upeyes, spikes can create fine inexpensive jewelry.

customized gemstones to make money."

This includes the customized work that he prefers. He finds that stone initials—these are great sellers!—work great with simple upeyes or glue-on pins. Because he cuts mostly custom and/or baroque shaped cabochons, Tom has a bit of trouble working them into standard pendants, pins and ear rings. It takes only a moment or two to properly drill a cabochon and then he can glue in a ringed post. Tom avoids the big Western gemstone buckles, but he does have a nice line of jeweled buckles suitable for everyday use.

"I always carry a wide range of one-of-a-kind ear rings. Women just love to look over ear rings. I use mostly surgical steel finds and try to have hundreds of selections. Many customers at a convention buy something right on the spot with the idea of wearing it immediately or later in the convention.

A woman can always use a new pair of ear rings. They're ab solutely the best on-the-spot sellers of all...no sizing...no nonsense

...and women don't need a sales job on ear rings. As a matter of fact, most women I sell to would resent a lot of sales talk. They can make up their own mind, thank you."

Makes Own Booth...

Tom saved money by making his own portable booth, one that would fold up and go into his car trunk. He sent away for literature from a California company that specializes in making small exhibit booths that fold into a suitcase size package.

He studied the pic tures carefully then retired

Idaho's Larry Gray displays attractively.

to his basement workshop. A few days later he had a beautiful table-top booth, that could be converted quickly into a full length standing booth. With her knowledge of fabrics and colors, Donna soon had the booth looking better than most professional jobs. Furthermore, the booth was designed to accept the Brissel's display trays. Tom set up the booth shelves so they would buckle from the back, using Velcro fastening material on the front. Some judicious use of fluroescent paint gave it a modern, trendy appearance that spelled profits.

To build business at the convention—most convention managers prohibit Tom from "working" the lobbies and convention floor—Tom has printed up "specials" slips three to a sheet. The convention manager will generally allow him to put a pile of these pricing slips on the registration desks out front and at strategic spots around the exhibit hall.

Selling convention may involve finished jewelry for best results, but many gemcutters are now considering the Jewelers of America convention shows and similar type shows where loose stone buyers are found.

As a ploy for building interest in his stones, Tom offers a special nice piece of jewelry and a discount on some of the items. This is intended to bring in traffic and build good will. At the convention, Tom is particularly careful about avoiding any blue suede shoe selling: people detest the hard sell at a convention. The word gets around quickly that Tom has fine, top quality, authentic jewelry at good prices. Everyone likes a bargain.

Beads and acorn pearls (fresh water pearls!) are also excellent convention sellers. Tom doesn't have the time or inclination to cut small beads so he buys them already strung from a wholesaler. He doesn't try to sell beads at a rock and gem show (too many Oriental dealers with better prices).

The Brissels do about a half dozen conventions a year, plus the Tucson show. If it's close enough and they have the time, Tom and Donna will schedule in a rock and gem show or a local mineral show. The latter shows aren't especially lucrative so they've been minimizing them. They ignore craft shows where everyone is selling their own brand of jewelry. Of course, Tom has been known to attend a craft show with his loaded brief cases and search for loose stone buyers. The New Orleans pair also avoid flea markets and swap meets where jewelry makes a powerful presence.

Straight Approach to Trade...

Tom admits he prefers selling to the jewelry trade. The buyers are knowledgeable, have a good idea of what they want, know what they'll do with a gemstone, and have a firm idea of how much they're willing to pay.

"Sometimes I get into a bit of price negotiating but I generally don't overprice anyway so there's no reason to allow myself to be chiseled down. A person in the trade knows what keystone is and realizes that I have to live, too.

"It's the outright chiseler that gets my goat sometimes. But my prices aren't writ in stone. I'll negotiate if I must to avoid losing

Your first moments with a buyer will usually determine whether or not you'll sell a stone. Work hard to demonstrate honesty, knowledge and sincerely.

the sale," Tom admits.

He visits his best customers once every three months or so. From time to time, too, he gives them a call if he has some interesting material that he believes a particular artisan will be interested in. Tom keeps a card history on each customer and has a complete record of what he or she has bought from him, likes, dislikes, design notions..that kind of thing.

"It's important to have good records on your customers," he says. "And they appreciate it, too, that you have a good line on them...that you don't bother them with things that they've already warned you off on."

The Brissels are moving to modern hi-tech, too. Their 3x5 card file has been moved to a hand-held Sharp computer and now Tom can update and retrieve any of his customers in a flash.

"You can't imagine how valuable this little computer has become. I now have all my customers a key punch away. I have my stone inventory and show schedule on it. In short my whole business is stored in this little machine—and I have memory enough to store ten more businesses like mine in it. The nice thing, I'm never going to the office supply store anymore to buy cards and paper. It's simply amazing, and I'd recommend one for every gemcutter in America, hobbyist or professional."

Tom summarizes his successful marketing plan this way.

"You know, if a gemcutter is cutting an expensive piece of material, he or she will take each step one at a time, in sequence, and work diligently at each step before going on to the next. A good polish—the successful conclusion—to a gemcutting operation depends on the skill of all of the previous cutting steps and how you've brought them together.

"Selling is like that, too. You have to take each step one at a time and do it right, too. You have to have a plan, good display or presentation tools, effective literature and promotional materials, and your own personality and sales attitude. A completed sale—the successful conclusion—to a marketing plan depends on the attention and skill with which you've addressed all the previous steps and how you've brought them together.

Both gemcutting and selling take time, preparation, and follow through.

Some Final Considerations...

Regardless of the size of your operation or whether or not it's home based, you should know that you may be subject to local, state, and federal laws and rules. Before you get too far into your business plan, contact a lawyer or local authorities.

Some communities prohibit certain kinds of home businesses in a residential neighborhood while others give considerable leeway to commercial ventures. It's no fun to launch a business and get it off to a promising start only to encounter unexpected difficulties concerning zoning, liability regulations, home deliveries, and licensing. Likewise the county and state government will want to know about your business (they'll invariably have some taxation regulations governing your activities.).

If your efforts will include only a sale or two or a student in the den, workshop or basement now and then you probably won't need the assistance of a lawyer, an accountant, a banker and an insurance representative. Should your business get really active or begin to show promise, get counsel quickly from a lawyer familiar with business and corporation law. Then hold meetings with the other professionals.

These people make their living advising and keeping business people on the path to success. Your success is their success. Don't forgo their valuable advice and contributions. All the how-to books in the world usually won't provide the localized information that professional people in your own community can offer.

Marketing Opportunities: Selling to Other Lapidaries

Not all marketing opportunities exist outside of the lapidary field. Some of the best profit making ventures consist of products or services that other gemcutters would be interested in purchasing.

By selling your own products and services to your colleagues you can make a tidy profit—if the idea is a good one. After all, in the great Gold Rush Days in California, it was not the prospectors who made all the great fortunes: it was the wily merchants who sold the picks and shovels to the miners.

The "Easy Way"...

Don Clark, of Yreka, CA, is a good example of a gemcutter who experiences a commendable income. Don noted that many gemcutters get tangle up with all the precise meet point obligations of faceting. They all want an easier way, Don reasoned. So he came up with a system called the EASY WAY.

The EASY WAY involves a remarkably simple procedure for cutting complex faceted shapes with a minimum of difficulty. Don knew that preforming the shape of a faceted design represented no great difficulty for most faceters. If a faceter can figure out his or her own design, then the problem is virtually completed.

Once the girdle is done, Don figured out a consistent way that

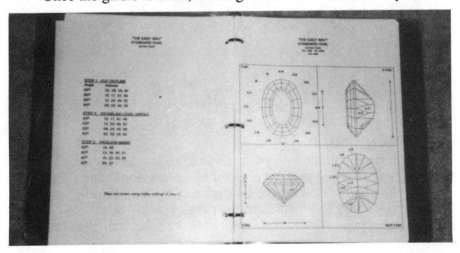

a row of pavilion facets could be cut into the 90 degree girdle so that the design shape would be maintained while forming an even girdle line. Once this first row of defining pavilion facets were cut it, Don figured the main facets could be cut at the proper angle and the pavilion would be finished. With the pavilion complete, Don's EASY WAY system calls for a step-cut crown—and PRESTO!—the faceted stone is finished.

Once he had his system worked out, Don wrote up a book of instructions, developed a series of designs that a beginner could work on. The next step was to introduce his copyrighted system to the faceting world. This he did by running classified ads in American Gemcutter, official magazine of the American Society of Gemcutters (he got the first test ad free because he is a member). Encouraged by his test, Don rolled out with a six-month program of classified ads for a total investment of $60.

Here is a copy of the small ad that Don runs:

> **MODERN FACETING: "The Easy Way"** Comprehensive new book covers almost every shape and proportioned gem. New techniques to increase yield while cutting for maximum brilliance that are INCREDIBLY EASY! $24.99 ppd. The Gem Garden, 400 Hiram Page #50, Yreka, CA 96097

The EASY WAY system really works. It saves a lot of mental anguish when faceting a tough design. If you are interested in obtaining a copy of Don's personalized EASY WAY course, write to him at:

Don Clark
The Gem Garden
400 Hiram Page rd., #50
Yreka, CA 96097

The Magic of mAgi

Earlier in this book, you read an excellent article on selling by Rick Ford. Rick is the proprietor of a marvelous little company in Oregon that specializes in selling faceting and cabbing supplies, rough including Montana sapphire rough alongwith a line of highly effective special colloidal polishes used with Moyco Ultra Laps.

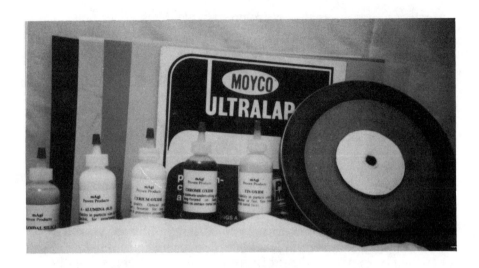

These mAgi colloidal oxide polishes represent high-tech polishing, especially when used in conjunction with Moyco's Ultra laps.

Rick is a professional faceter. He also has developed the touch for cutting those thin, small, high quality Montana sapphires. But he long ago discovered the way to extra income would be to provide a valuable service to other faceters. As a result, he organized mAgi and began promoting a number of fine products.

If you wish to buy Montana sapphire rough (and every American gemcutter should cut at least ONE Montana sapphire) while talking to a top professional faceter about this type of crystal. then Rick is probably one of the best to deal with. He can converse with and advise you on cutting just about any gem crystal but it's with Montana sapphire that he has earned a reputation for expertise.

Because consistent oxide polishes are tough to obtain, Rick recently completed R&D on an entire line of colloidal chemical oxide polishes. The only person in the country who offers colloidal oxide polishes—including the new, amazing colloidal silica polish—Rick now has a fine repeat business for gemcutters who prefer a consistently wetted, pre-mixed polish. What makes colloidal polish different and remain superior to powder polishes is the consistent suspension of oxide particles in a wet solution.This makes polishing so much easier and so much more predictable. Rick encourages the use of vinegar (ascetic acid) to accelerate polishing action of colloidals.

Also, if you need a small display case to carry your gems around and have them available, Rick also sells a beautiful hand made leather case (made by master saddlemaker Jerk (sic) Steiner of Montana). If you'd like to contact Rick, write to:

> mAgi
> PO Box 426
> Beavercreek, OR 97004

On Transfer and Dopping Blocks...

Don Cook of Omaha, NE, a retired railroad engineer, has been making a steady income off his gemcutting hobby for years.

Cutting commercial level gemstones and selling them for profit has long been part of the profit formula for this Nebraska native.

Don Cook's 3-dop transfer block accepts multiple dops for production cutters, and the dopping blocks, depending on size, hold up to 250 dop sticks.

Especially since his retirement, Don has been turning out a steady stream of competent faceters. He runs his classrooms right in his own home workshop.

Lately, he took up metal machining and now makes--and sells to faceters—a beautiful aluminum multiple post transfer block, for transferring a half cut stone to the remaining half for cutting. What makes the Cook transfer block so unusual is its readiness to accept a number of dopping sticks at the same time. Such a tool is invaluable to a professional cutter who'made facet a series of stones and doesn't wish to perform the transfer dopping function in sequence.

In his workshop,too, Don makes magnificent hardwood dopping blocks...a block with a series of holes drilled into it which entertain the quarter-inch dopping sticks used by faceters for holding their cut stones.

Don promotes his teaching operation locally, depending on word-of-mouth from satisfied graduates. He went national with his aluminum transfer block and the varieties of wooden dopping stick holder blocks. He ran space display ads in American Gemcutter Magazine, supported by a series of classified ads.

If you'd like to receive information on these fine products that Don makes himself, write to:

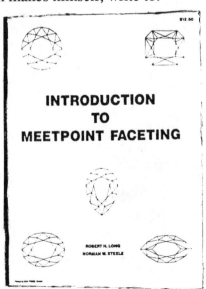

Cook's Enterprises
205 South 15th
Norfolk, NE 68701

Pages and Pages of Designs

The one thing that a practicing faceter likes to obtain is another design.

Recognizing this desire, Normal Steele Jr. and Bob Long, a pair of engineers from Washington state, latched onto the meet point faceting breakthrough with a series of design books. Their books, printed in large 8.5"x11" 3-ring booklets, are extremely popular among the world's faceting community.

If another design shows up anywhere in the industry press, Norm and Bob get busy with cutting instructions and corrections and include them in their newsletter and/or new book.

The popular authors, using hand calculators, paved the way for computerized cutting instructions. Their pioneering work won the 1993 Crystalite Award, given by the American Society of Gemcutters to the individual(s) who have made the greatest contribution to gemcutting. Norm and Bob have published five books of designs and each one represents an enormous fund of useful information.

At one time, the pair advertised their books in the national lapidary trade press. In the past few years, the books have become so well known that press comment is sufficient—and easy availability in the nation's rock shops—to keep sales flowing.

If you are interested in contacting the authors' publishing company about *Facet Design* books, call or write:

Seattle Facet Books
2232 - 78 Av SE
Mercer Island, WA 98040

Getting a Line on Prices...

Any gemcutter who wishes to cut and sell his or her work must have a reasonably good line on current prices.

Sofus Michelsen, a certified master cutter from Bayonne, NJ, saw the need for a good, reliable pricing service that also dispensed with valuable gemological information. In the late 80's, Sofus

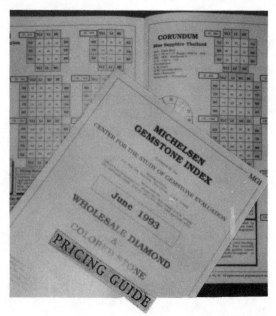

launched his pricing guide. It quickly became successful among professional cutters and gem buyers. Published in New Jersey, Gemstone Index enjoys a reputation as one of the country's more dependable guides—with lots of useful gem lore and information.

Sofus' guide has always been directed toward both gemcutter and jewelers use. He keeps a careful tab on what cutters charge their retail cutters so any gemcutter could quickly get a quick line on any stone. The newsletter is set up to emphasize certain stones each report so a year's subscription consisting of four editions would pretty much cover the entire spectrum of commercially cut gemstones.

ASG Gemstone Monthly Pricing Tab		
Colored Stones		
	Ruby	180-3370
3-9	Sapphire	125-1630
.55-1.60	**Garnet**	
18-30	Rhodolite	12-25
380-3235	Almandine	11-27
114-260	Hessonite	7-36
	Malaya	30-130
24-68	Tsavorite	38-175
85-645	**Iolite**	1-10
85-1300	**Jade**	
2-105	Jadeite	25-308
	Nephrite	3-167
4-12	**Kunzite**	9-260
120-400	**Lapis**	2-225
2-9	**Malachite**	3-37
	DIAMONDS	
	Size	

You can't get enough pricing data.
The American Society of Gemcutters
also publishes a monthly price guide.

If you are interested in details about this fine pricing service, call or write:

Center For Study of Gemstone Evaluation
PO Box 195
Bayonne, NJ 07002
1-800-648-4367

Other Entrepreneurs in Lapidary...

A number of other entrepreneurs have developed good income businesses by turning their efforts to the lapidary community.

They others include California's Fred Van Zandt who develops and sells faceting designs; Robert W. Strickland of Austin, TX, developer of the highly regarded GemCad and GemTrace software programs which enables design minded people to come up with their own faceting designs and instructions and optics analysis; Clint Fruitman, formerly of Tucson, AZ, who developed and sold the Ultima cut and was at one time ready to launch a synthetic crystal growing business.

Other successful lapidary suppliers include author John Zinkankas of San Diego, CA, who has written a number of fine books for lapidaries; California's Glen Vargas, author of "Faceting For Amateurs," and Edward J. Soukup of San Diego, author of the excellent "Facet Cutters Handbook."

At one time, a number of people were promoting their own design of "automatic cabochon dopsticks" but lately little is noted of promotional activity for these devices. About the only unique tool is the "PreFormer" sold by Rick Ford of mAgi. The Preformer is a tool invented by the same Phil Bean of Seattle, WA, who also developed and marketed the original Fac-Ette faceting machine.

Many successful lapidary entrepeneurs have made a profitable success of developing products and services for other gemcutters. Any good idea has a potential market—and it doesn't cost that much to test market your idea.

This section does not include the number of small lapidary businesses that men and women conduct, selling rough, laps, and other supplies. Many of these entrepreneurs run classified ads regularly in the lapidary press. While their businesses may or may not make a high income, many of the ads continue to run month after month. This at least indicates that some income is being realized from their efforts.

So if you have an idea for a new tool or device that lapidaries can use, work up your idea and develop a test marketing plan. This can be as simple as sitting down and writing a small classified ad and then contacting a publication that lapidaries read.

Should you prepare an inventory in case the product takes off?

Most of the time, investing in inventory prior to knowing how well your idea will do is not a good option. It costs valuable promotional money to promote, and your first efforts should be to develop a customer list. If you get more orders than you can immediately accommodate, a quick note to buying customers that there will be a slight delay because orders exceeded inventory. With most people, this polite notification will suffice—and they will be willing to wait for a reasonable period.

Once you've bought yourself some time, get busy and build enough inventory to satisfy YOUR IMMEDIATE ORDERS. Again, don't go investing in inventory until you've gone through the test marketing plan three times. By that time, you'll have a good idea how many orders you will receive for your level of promotion.

The one thing you want to be in position for is a roll out should your early promotional efforts indicate that you probably have a hit. If a classified ad in one magazine pays for itself and makes a few extra dollars, your immediate response should be to run an ad in another magazine...not produce extra inventory. Use the money to promote, not build parts. That may sound like strange advice but, believe me, it will save you a lot of money and heartbreak. There's no more painful outcome than a would-be entrepreneur who made sure he had lots of products before he made sure he had lots of customers. Cellars and basements are filled with unsuccessful business adventures where the initial money stake was spent improperly in the beginning. Get the customer first. That's where the incoming money comes from. Inventory is where the money goes out—and that's the last investment you should make.

Appendix A

CONSIGNMENT AGREEMENT

Consignment agreement made this   date of   by and between   (Consignor)
and   (Undersigned)

1. Undersigned acknowledges receipt of gemstones as described on attached schedule. Said goods shall remain property of Consignor until sold or returned
2. The Undersigned at its own cost and expense agrees to keep and display the goods only in its place of business, and agrees, on demand made before any sale, to return the same in good order and condition.
3. The Undersigned agrees to use its best efforts to sell the goods for the Consignor's account on cash terms, and at such prices as shall from time to time be designated by Consignor
4. The Undersigned agrees, upon sale, to maintain proceeds due Consignor in trust, and separate and apart from its own funds and deliver such proceeds, less commission, to Consignor together with an accounting within   days of said sale.
5. The Undersigned agrees to accept as full payment a commission equal to   % of the gross sales price exclusive of any sales tax, which the Undersigned shall collect and remit.
6. The Undersigned agrees to sell said gemstones at prices that have been agreed upon and appear on the aforesaid attached schedule.
6. The Undersigned agrees to permit the Consignor to enter the premises at reasonable times to examine and inspect the goods, and reconcile an accounting of sums

due.

7. The Undersigned agrees to issue such financing state-
ments for public filing as may reasonably be required
by Consignor.

8. This agreement shall be binding upon and inure to the
benefit of the parties, their successors and assigns.

_____   _____
(Consignor)   (Undersigned)

REPAIR WORK

(Author's Note: Most repair work is accepted "on honor"
with the repairman writing down the work to be done on the work
envelope, noting any gemstones, and a receipt issued to the custom-
er.)

Note: It is critical that a repairman never write down
the identity of a valuable gemstone without first examining
the stone in a laboratory and making a definitive identification. In
the absence of such a careful analysis, note only that
you are accepting a

"red stone"   instead of "ruby, rubellite, etc."
"blue stone"   instead of "sapphires, tanzanite, etc."
"white stone" instead of "diamond, etc."

Below is the type of agreement you might want to use with
customers who request a bid on your work or who might turn over
an expensive or complex piece of jewelry for repair.

REPAIR WORK AGREEMENT

TO:

ADDRESS:

CITY   STATE   ZIP

Dear Sir:

_____will furnish all materials and per-
form all labor necessary to complete the following

        All of the above lapidary and/or jewelry work will be
completed in a substantial and workmanlike manner according to standard lapidary practices or applicable codes for the
sum of Dollars ($)
        Any alteration or modification from the above specifica-
tions involving extra cost of material or time will only be executed upon written orders from same, and will become an extra charge over the sum mentioned in this contract. All
agreements must be made in writing.
                        Respectfully Submitted,

                By

        ACCEPTANCE
                You are hereby authorized to funish all materials and
labor required to complete the work mentioned in the above proposal, for which
agrees to pay the amount contained in said proposal, and according
to the terms thereof.
                ACCEPTED   _____
                        Date:_____

Appendix B

HELPFUL BOOKS, MAGAZINES AND NEWSLETTERS

The U. S. Small Business Administration (SBA) was created by Congress to provide aid and support of small businesses. Besides financial assistance, SBA offers a wide ranging low-cost as well as a free publications program.

You can order a free catalog, or any of the publications listed below, by writing to:

> SBA
> PO Box 15434
> Fort Worth, TX 76119.

Make your check or money order payable to U. S. Small Business Administration. Keep in mind that booklet prices change regularly.

Accounting Services for Small Service Firms (FM 6) $0.50

Advertising (MT 11) $1.00

Business Plan for Small Manufacturers (MP 4) $1.00

Evaluating Franchise Opportunities (MP 26) $1.00

Going into Business (MP 12) $0.50

Ideas into Dollars (PI 1) $2.00

Planning and Goal Setting for Small Business (MP 6) $0.50

Pricing Your Products and Services Profitably (FM 13) $1.00

Record Keeping in a Small Business (FM 10) $1.00

Selecting the Legal Structure for Your Business (MP 25) $1.00

Understanding Cash Flow (FM 4) $1.00

Some other independent books and magazines that will help you on the subject of starting up a small lapidary business include:

Books
The Where-to-Sell-It-Directory, by Margaret Boyd, Pilot Books, Babylon, NJ 1990

Selling Skills for the Non-Salesperson: For People Who Hate to Sell, But Love to Succeed, by Gary S. Goodman, Prentice-Hall, Englewood Cliffs, NJ 1984

The Flea Market Entrepreneur, by Charlotte Harmona, Pilot Books

Running a One Person Business, by Claude Whitmeyer, Salli Rasberry, and Michael Phillips, Ten Speed Press, Berkeley, CA 1989

On Your Own: A Woman's Guide to Building a Business, by Laurie Zuckerman, Upstart of Dover, NJ   1990

You Can Make Money from Your Arts and Crafts, by Steve and Cindy Long, Mark Publications, Scotts Valley, CA 1988

Magazines
Entrepreneur, 2392 Morse av., Irvine, CA 92714

Inc., 38 commercial Wharf, Boston, MA 02110

Success (Incorporating Success Unlimited), 230 Park av., New York, NY 10169

Index

Other Books
by
Gerald L.Wykoff GG CSM

Beyond the Glitter   **$17.95   Hardcover**
   A comprehensive review of gem and jewelry knowledge. This criti-
cally acclaimed book won't make you a professional gemologist, but
you'll enable you to hold your own with any professional

The Techniques of Master Faceting $24.50   Hardcover
   Regarded by most as the "bible" of the faceting world, this book is
the most comprehensive book ever written on colored stone faceting—plus diamond cutting. It's a book of instructions like no other.

The Techniques of Master Stonesetting $24.50   Hardcover
   Every possible technique and method for setting gemstones in described in words and the more than 1000 illustrations. It covers tools,
techniques, gemstone characteristics, opticals and metal finishing.

Master Jewelry Design and Creation $24.50   Hardcover
   Now you can learn to come up with jewelry design ideas and then
use the metal working methods to bring your concepts to life. Includes a revolutionary, easy way to make jewelry using dental products.

Master Gemcutting Tips   **$14.95   Paperback**
   A comprehensive compilation of gemcutting techniques and methods
used by hobbyists and professionals. If you have a question about
gemcutting, chances are the answers will be found in this paperback.

If you would like one of Gerald Wykoff's above books, order from:

Adamas Publishers
PO Box 1991
York, PA 17405
1-717-741-2469

(Please add $3 to your order for postage and handling)